DEREK JETER

DEREK

JETER

FROM THE PAGES OF
The New York Times

INTRODUCTION BY TYLER KEPNER

ABRAMS, NEW YORK

"I can't tell you how much I admire Derek Jeter, everything about him. He's a symbol of everything that's right about the game, as far as I'm concerned. He's a great role model for other players. When I tell my kids or grandkids about the great players from my time, I'll be proud to say I was on the same field with Derek Jeter."

HOWIE KENDRICK of the Los Angeles Angels, *Sept. 11, 2009*

CONTENTS

INTRODUCTION

DEREK JETER

by Tyler Kepner

Derek Jeter grew up in Kalamazoo, Mich., next to a baseball field. Every day, just behind his backyard, it was there, calling him to play. And so he did, and he has never stopped.

Jeter wrote a book once, with the former New York Times baseball writer Jack Curry, called "The Life You Imagine." The title was perfect, especially if "you" signifies every child who has picked up a baseball and dreamed. To be sure, there are things we do not know about Jeter's life, details he guards closely. But he has lived nearly all of his adult years as a baseball celebrity in New York, and what we know still reads like a fairy tale, the kind we want to believe is still possible in sports.

Derek Jeter scores the third Yankees run of the seventh inning in Game 2 of the American League Division Series against the Minnesota Twins, *Oct. 2, 2003.*
Photo: Barton Silverman,
The New York Times

He was raised in a loving home by an African-American father and a white mother. He was born in New Jersey and rooted for the Yankees, because that was his grandmother's team. He was the best high school player in the country as a senior, and the Yankees — drafting high in 1992 because they had finished so poorly the year before — selected and signed him.

Skinny and raw, alone in the minor leagues, he made errors prodigiously and cried to his parents over the telephone at night. But he forged deep friendships, with Jorge Posada and Mariano Rivera and Andy Pettitte, and moved to Tampa, Fla., so he could be close to the Yankees' minor league complex and training site.

Before his 21st birthday, he was playing shortstop at Yankee Stadium. The next year, he won the World Series, the first title for his boyhood team since he was four years old. He won the Rookie of the Year award and started a foundation that has raised millions to keep children off drugs.

In an age when players routinely change teams, he stayed with the Yankees and became their captain. He won the most championships and dated the prettiest starlets and, eventually, compiled more hits for the Yankees than any player who ever lived. The previous record belonged to another Yankees captain, Lou Gehrig, an iconic name in American history.

By the time he passed Gehrig, Jeter had become the face of the most decorated franchise in sports, with unmistakable appeal across gender and racial lines. Even Red Sox fans respected him. Before the first game of the 2009 World Series, he looked regal and respectful as he escorted the first lady, Michelle Obama, to the field for the ceremonial first pitch. The next night, he looked carefree and hip, bopping his head in the dugout as Jay-Z and Alicia Keys performed on a stage in the outfield.

The song was "Empire State of Mind," an anthem to New York City, and Jeter adopted it as his own, asking that it be played before some of his at-bats at the new Yankee Stadium, the $1.5 billion castle his excellence helped build. When Jeter played his first game at the old Stadium, on June 2, 1995, there were 16,959 people in the stands. By 2008, when the building closed, the Yankees averaged more than 53,000 per game.

Jeter did not do it alone, not at all. He came along at precisely the right time in precisely the right era, when the Yankees' hard-driving owner, George Steinbrenner, was banned from baseball for paying a gambler to find damaging information on Dave Winfield, Jeter's childhood hero. With Steinbrenner's influence dulled, the Yankees developed and retained the core of young players who would form the foundation of the team's return to glory. Wise trades and signings, supported by Steinbrenner's financial muscle, filled out the rest.

Along the way, the Yankees went global, expanding their footprint by taking the team to Japan and sending scouts and executives to China. They beamed their product to the masses on their own cable network, and their overflowing revenue streams included the new Stadium and reflected an annual budget that defiantly exceeds the collectively bargained limit for tax-free team payrolls.

Jeter, who wants to own a team someday, would have it no other way. He was part of the last generation of Yankees to know the feisty Steinbrenner, before the owner's health deteriorated in the first decade of the new century. At one point, Jeter took a tabloid broadside from Steinbrenner, who chastised him for supposedly partying too much. With typical good humor — and keen financial sense — Jeter and Steinbrenner ended up spoofing their dispute in a commercial for Visa.

Steinbrenner, who died in July 2010, was famous for motivational exhortations, some of them corny and laughable to the modern player. Many sayings are splashed on large white signs in the tunnels leading to the home clubhouse in spring training, including one that has just one word: "Accountability." Jeter may not be inspired by those signs, but he lives that trait.

For years, when Manager Joe Torre was asked about Jeter, he would cite Jeter's rookie season, in 1996. Although Torre had named him the starting shortstop before spring training, Jeter refused to say the job was his, only that he had an opportunity to win it. It was more than a semantic distinction; to Torre, it was a sign of maturity. The kid knew not to take things for granted. He had a magnetism that made veterans want to follow his example, and his age was irrelevant. Only 21, Jeter was a grown-up.

When he made an error, it was not Jeter's way to berate himself on the field or grouse in the dugout. When the Yankees came off the field, Jeter would simply take a seat beside Torre, a silent acknowledgment that he had messed up and would accept the ramifications. Torre would smile and wave him off.

It was a tenet of Jeter's credo: a ballplayer should admit a physical error, but not apologize. Mistakes happen, as Jeter knew all too acutely. In 1993, his first full professional season, he made 56 errors for Class A Greensboro. After intensive off-season practice, he was hailed by Baseball America as the game's best prospect a year later.

"You knew that he was special," Pettitte said, on the night Jeter broke Gehrig's hits record, in 2009. "You knew that he carried himself a little bit different than a lot of other guys, a lot of class, a lot of charisma, a lot of confidence for as young as he was."

His path to becoming team captain began before he reached the majors, after a spring training workout in Fort Lauderdale, Fla., when Don Mattingly told him to run — not walk — off the field at a seemingly deserted ballpark. "You never know who's watching," Mattingly said, and since then Jeter has lived

Jeter acknowledges the cheers after tying Lou Gehrig's record for hits as a Yankee, *Sept. 9, 2009.*
Photo: Richard Perry, The New York Times

by those words. When he is in public, he understands people could be watching.

Told once that another Yankee captain, Thurman Munson, was often churlish to reporters, Jeter smiled and said, "You mean I don't have to talk to you guys?" But he does talk, every day, and the spotlight never seems to be a burden. From Torre and David Cone, a star pitcher on four Yankees title teams, Jeter learned that it is much easier to deal with reporters than to avoid them.

His style is to be approachable and unflappable. He nods a lot and smiles a little, and he will make small talk if you want; his favorite topic is college sports, and the University of Michigan in particular. His answers are concise and consistent. He rarely admits to an injury and never concedes that a physical problem affects his play. He disdains talking about individual achievement, and rejects the idea that one game is any bigger than another. If the Jeter quote machine had a default setting, it would be: "The bottom line is winning."

He does not believe he should tell fans how to act, a stance that became a flashpoint in 2006, when Jeter would not admonish fans for booing the struggling Alex Rodriguez. He will not discuss his romantic life. He will not criticize a teammate or speak for someone else. "You'd have to ask him" is another standard response.

Reporters sometimes complain that Jeter is boring, and in some ways, his answers are; he does not ruminate or speak anecdotally. But if you ask a direct question, he usually gives a direct answer. And because Jeter is so reliably available, reporters know they can always get the voice of the Yankees' captain into their stories — no small thing, especially on deadline.

Jeter does not delve too deeply into hitting theory and, with a few exceptions — notably Roy Halladay and the longtime reliever Mike Timlin — rarely admits that a pitcher is generally difficult to hit. As always, he would rather give simple answers that say a lot. When he hits the ball the opposite way, Jeter will say, it is usually a fastball. When he turns on a pitch and pulls it, it is usually a breaking ball or a changeup. It takes Hall of Fame-level pitch recognition, reflexes and confidence to wait on every pitch the way Jeter does, but when he speaks about hitting, he makes it seem easy.

There is also this: Jeter will never allow himself to be burned by a reporter. In my eight years as the Yankees' beat writer for The Times, he never once asked to talk off the record. He puts his name behind everything he says. Accountability, again.

Jeter never raises his voice in the clubhouse, unless he is calling across the room for Posada to wrap up an interview. "Sado!" he shouts, repeating a nickname he gave the Yankees catcher in the 1995 playoffs, when the public-address announcer, Bob Sheppard, mistakenly announced him as "Posado."

Yet Jeter is appropriately reverential of Sheppard, who formally retired in 2009 (and died in 2010), concluding a career that began in 1951, Mickey Mantle's rookie season. Jeter insisted that as long as he plays, Sheppard's recorded voice will introduce him when he comes to bat. That is one link Jeter brought from the old Yankee Stadium to the new one. Another is his number, 2. Every other single-digit number besides 6 (worn by Torre) was retired before the Yankees moved.

Jeter was raised on Yankees history. He sometimes watched the Yankees in person when they visited Detroit, and on summer trips back east to see his grandmother. Usually he watched the Yankees on television, listening to their old shortstop, Phil Rizzuto, call the games.

When Rizzuto died in 2007, Jeter revealed that the only autograph he owns is one by Rizzuto, on a photograph of them together. Because he does not care much for mementos, the ones Jeter keeps are significant. When the old Stadium was gutted, Jeter asked for one item: the sign that hung in the runway from the clubhouse to the dugout, emblazoned with a Joe DiMaggio quote from 1949: "I want to thank the Good Lord for making me a Yankee."

The old Stadium was the players' stage, and that is how Jeter described it at the end. He would say that he had never been on Broadway, but he guessed that the angles and the contours and the lighting made it feel the same. Certainly, in the baseball sense, he had experienced comedy, triumph and tragedy under those lights.

Early in his rookie season, 1996, he squeezed the final out of Dwight Gooden's no-hitter. Five months later, in a playoff game against the Orioles, he punched a deep fly ball to right field that a young fan, Jeffrey Maier, deflected into the stands. It was ruled a home run, and the Yankees would win the game. They soon celebrated their 23rd championship, and Jeter's first.

Five more times, the Yankees would clinch a pennant or a championship with a victory at the old Stadium, including the 2000 A.L. crown, ensuring a World Series matchup with the crosstown Mets. In Game 1, Jeter made a pivotal throw to nail Timo Perez at the plate, putting the Yankees in position to tie the game in the ninth and win it in extra innings.

The Yankees won the next night, but the Mets took Game 3 at Shea Stadium. The fourth game was their chance to build off that momentum, but it did not last one pitch. Leading off the game, Jeter drilled Bobby Jones's first-pitch changeup over the left-center-field wall, seizing control of the Series for good. It was, perhaps, the single most emphatic symbol of the Yankees' dominance of that era: *Nice try, but we'll take it from here.*

In 2001, Jeter ushered in November baseball with a homer to win Game 4 of the World Series against the Arizona Diamondbacks. The cameras went right to his parents, Charles and Dorothy, overjoyed in the rollicking stands. Three games later, Jeter was covering second base in the ninth inning of Game 7, with the Yankees leading by a run, ready to catch a throw from Rivera for a force-out. But Rivera threw away the rain-slicked ball, setting in motion the Diamondbacks' winning rally.

That loss touched off a string of eight consecutive seasons in which the Yankees did not win the World Series. By any other team's definition, that stretch would have been a source of pride, because the Yankees still reached the playoffs seven times. They also captured the 2003 A.L. pennant with a spine-tingling victory over Boston in Game 7 of the championship series; Jeter doubled over right fielder Trot Nixon's head to spark the pivotal comeback off Pedro Martinez. But the so-called Steinbrenner Doctrine, fully endorsed and perpetuated by Jeter, made it all unfulfilling.

Steinbrenner believed that a season without a World Series title was a failure, and Jeter adopted the mantra as his own. It was consistent with his internal wiring. Jeter, like Steinbrenner, has never understood the concept of a moral victory. The object of the game is to win, and unless you win the World Series, you've failed to reach your goal. Victories are victories, and they are all great. Losses are losses, and all of them hurt.

The loss in the 2003 World Series, to a young Florida Marlins team that had not even finished in first place in its division, was a bitter blow to owner and captain. It took the acquisition of the so-called best player in baseball, on the eve of spring training, to lift Steinbrenner's spirits. The player, of course, was Rodriguez, obtained from the Texas Rangers for Alfonso Soriano and the minor league infielder Joaquin Arias. (In a bit of good fortune for the Yankees, Texas chose Arias over Robinson Cano, who would become an All-Star and Jeter's longest-running double-play partner.)

In deference to Jeter, Rodriguez switched to third base from shortstop, where he had just won two Gold Gloves and was widely regarded as a stronger fielder. Jeter could make the snazzy jump throw from deep in the shortstop hole, but Rodriguez's arm was far superior, without the style points. He was the reigning Most Valuable Player and a prodigious run producer, seemingly destined to make the Yankees better. But he had a complicated history with Jeter.

I first interviewed Jeter in the late 1990's, while covering the Mariners for The Seattle Post-Intelligencer. It was brief, just a question or two. I really don't remember much about it, but I do remember Rodriguez's reaction.

Rodriguez was the Mariners' shortstop then, precocious and polished, a year younger than Jeter but otherwise his peer.

▲ The Jeter family — Dorothy, Derek, Sharlee and Charles — before the start of the last game at the old Yankee Stadium, *Sept. 21, 2008.*
Photo: Jim McIsaac, Getty Images

◄ The sign is now Jeter's most treasured souvenir from the original Yankee Stadium.
Photo: Mark Lennihan, Associated Press

Jeter and Alex Rodriguez
of the Seattle Mariners in
August 1996 — the early
days of a long, complicated
relationship.
Photo: Diamond Images/
Getty Images

Their lives and careers would diverge greatly, but at the time they seemed to have much in common. They were high school phenoms in the early 1990's and rookie shortstops in 1995, when their teams faced each other in the first round of the American League playoffs.

Jeter quickly began collecting championship rings on Broadway, while Rodriguez compiled better statistics in the faraway Northwest. For Rodriguez, Jeter was a friend but also a source of fascination, and when I casually mentioned that we had spoken, Rodriguez eagerly asked my impression.

"He's a little like you," I said, and though I later learned this to be terribly inaccurate, at the time it seemed to delight Rodriguez, who smiled broadly and pushed for specifics. It was just a glint of what so many people in their orbits would recognize: that Rodriguez aspired to be like Jeter, often with a kind of jealous desperation.

Their facade of similarity disappeared when Rodriguez accepted a 10-year, $252 million contract from the Texas Rangers after losing the 2000 A.L.C.S. to the Yankees. The deal enriched Jeter, too, the rising salary tide forcing the Yankees to give him his own 10-year deal (for $189 million) that same off-season. But while Rodriguez became a mercenary, despised in Seattle for an audacious money grab, Jeter continued with his original team. Their underlying narratives hardened.

Rodriguez, for all his wondrous talents, seemed to complicate everything. Jeter's world was simple, his rules rigid. And when Rodriguez ripped Jeter in the April 2001 issue of Esquire, downplaying his impact in the Yankees' lineup and minimizing his leadership, it was a galling display of disloyalty that severely wounded their friendship. Rodriguez drove 95 miles to Jeter's home after the story was published, seeking forgiveness that was not forthcoming.

Jeter's grudge was a sign of his sensitivity, perhaps, a trait he also showed in 2003, when he refused to absolve a journeyman Toronto catcher, Ken Huckaby, for dislocating his shoulder in an accidental collision at third base. But in Rodriguez's case, the feud — or, more accurately, the cold war — was more personal, cutting deeper and exposing much about the character of both men, on and off the field.

Rodriguez had tried to promote himself by saying that, as a middle-of-the-order thumper, he was more imposing to other teams and somehow a better leader than Jeter. But comparisons to Jeter never really add up, because there is no way to quantify the glow — part real, part imagined — that Jeter brings to his team. And when the Yankees traded for Rodriguez, it served to elevate Jeter, not diminish him. Rodriguez was supposed to play Babe Ruth to Jeter's Gehrig, but for years he was more Goofus to Jeter's Gallant.

Goofus and Gallant are the characters in the magazine Highlights for Children who show precisely the right and wrong things to do in a given situation. Goofus leaves dirty plates for his parents to clean; Gallant grabs a dishrag — and so on. For five years, that was Rodriguez and Jeter. Rodriguez would fumble even the simplest act, while Jeter would be pitch-perfect. While Rodriguez dithered about which country to represent in the World Baseball Classic, for example, Jeter was promoted as the face of the United States team.

It was amusing to cover. Storms raged in Rodriguez's corner of the clubhouse, yet across the room Jeter's locker — next to the one left empty in Munson's memory — was a tranquil island. Rodriguez signed a contract loaded with perks, including a controversial out clause. Jeter's deal had no incentives. Rodriguez married before he was ready to settle down. Jeter stayed a bachelor. Rodriguez admitted to using steroids. Jeter insisted he was never tempted.

Their fundamental difference was self-assurance. Rodriguez projects insecurity while Jeter seems completely secure in who he is. Rodriguez's career has been marked by an ever-changing cast of mentors, advisers and image makers. Jeter surrounds himself with a fiercely loyal — and largely silent — group of family and friends he has known since childhood or his early professional career, like Posada and Gerald Williams.

f course, players on the same team do not have to be similar, and they do not have to be close friends. By the end of the 2000's, Jeter and Rodriguez had learned to function together — never close, but no longer icy. They had made different choices and discovered that they did not, in fact, have much in common except what mattered most: they were talented players who could help each other win.

Jeter's extraordinary self-confidence, perhaps as much as his fundamental skills, has helped him win more often than any other active player. For one reason or another, most talented players do not become stars. The players picked ahead of Jeter in the 1992 draft — Phil Nevin, Paul Shuey, B. J. Wallace, Jeffrey Hammonds and Chad Mottola — had forgettable careers, with just two appearances in the All-Star Game and none in the World Series. It was Jeter's fortune to be drafted by an ideal team, and his unshakable mind-set that allows his skills to flourish.

Jeter and Rodriguez tasted epic failure together before success. Jeter endured a stretch of 32 hitless at-bats in early 2004, a sign, some insisted, that he was burdened by Rodriguez's presence. Then again, Jeter produced the signature moment of that regular season with a face-first dive into the stands to snare a 12th-inning pop-up against the Red Sox. Bloodied in the face, Jeter rose from the stands as a grander, more mythic figure than ever; it was his finest moment since the off-balance infield flip that helped save an elimination game at Oakland in the 2001 playoffs.

Of course, the 2004 season ended with an unprecedented sting: four losses in a row to the Red Sox after taking a three-games-to-none lead in the A.L.C.S. Such a collapse had never happened in baseball history, yet the Red Sox, of all teams, did it to the Yankees to all but squash Ruth's curse.

The Yankees did not fall apart as a result, coming from behind to catch Boston in the 2005 regular season, but they seemed broken, wilting in the first round of the playoffs three years in a row and then, in 2008, missing them altogether for the first time in Jeter's career. Steadfastly that season, Jeter refused to acknowledge the obvious until the Yankees were mathematically out of it.

Symbolically, on the day the Yankees were eliminated, Jeter could not play because of soreness in his left hand, which had been hit by a pitch. He tried to take batting practice that night in Toronto, but he could not swing. Without their captain, the Yankees' playoff chances officially expired.

By then, though, Jeter had already had his moment. A few days earlier, he closed the final game at the original Stadium with a speech to the fans. The old guard of Rivera, Posada and Pettitte fanned out on either side of Jeter, with the rest of the team bunched behind them.

"We're relying on you to take the memories from this Stadium, add them to the new memories that come at the new Yankee Stadium, and continue to pass them on from generation to generation," he said. Jeter raised his cap to the crowd when he was through, and then delivered on the implied promise as quickly as possible.

In 2009, buoyed in part by a resurgent season from Jeter, the Yankees returned to the World Series and beat the Philadelphia Phillies in six games, clinching the championship at the new palace across 161st Street. Jeter led all players with 11 hits, matching the most for any player in a World Series since Jeter's rookie season.

"We play the game the right way," Jeter said on the podium, during the on-field celebration. "And we deserve to be standing here."

As he spoke, Jeter cradled the championship trophy. A widely used photo showed him clutching the prize, his right hand supporting it in back, his left hand supporting it underneath, the trophy nestled against his shirt as he held it out for Rivera to see. Jeter is smiling widely, beaming at a triumphant Rivera. He looks like a proud new parent, showing off his newborn.

Jeter has no children, but he often uses a parenting analogy when asked to compare one championship to another. The question is impossible to answer, Jeter says, as it would be for a father asked to pick his favorite child. They are all special in their own way, none more than any other.

The latest victory was Jeter's fifth — just five successful seasons, by his definition, in a long career. He used to talk about catching Yogi Berra's record of 10 World Series rings, a goal that seems unrealistic after the eight-year gap in the heart of his career. But Jeter will not dismiss it, and probably will not do so when he retires, either. He will find a loophole, a technicality — championships won as an owner, perhaps? — to make sure the game continues and that he is not defeated.

It is hard to imagine Jeter in retirement. He has yielded almost nothing to age, still playing a young man's position and working with a personal trainer to stay nimble — not that he would ever reveal the details of his preparation. He still bats high in the order, still posts the same kind of statistics, still has the same haircut.

Jeter's production slipped in 2010. Nobody in the majors made more outs, and Jeter's average, on-base percentage and slugging percentage all plunged to career lows for a full season. He looked ordinary in the postseason, which ended in an A.L.C.S. loss to Texas, and statisticians roundly mocked his Gold Glove award, citing ever-decreasing range.

Even so, Jeter's agent, Casey Close, entered the off-season seeking a contract that would reward his client for his iconic status. The Yankees insisted the negotiation be about baseball only, and they publicly expressed concerns about Jeter's age and performance, daring him to shop himself on the open market.

Those words wounded Jeter, he said, because he had told the Yankees privately that he never wanted to play anywhere else. In the end, the rancor subsided and Jeter signed a deal that guarantees him at least $51 million for three years and includes a player option for 2014. He will finish his career the way he started, a Yankee for life.

The decline of 2010 may be a blip on his stat sheet, or the start of an inevitable concession to age. But doubting Jeter has never been wise, and as he strives to remain among the game's elite, he has become a statesman for the younger generation.

The game marches on, with Jeter leading the way. At least two players — B. J. Upton and Troy Tulowitzki — have worn his No. 2 because they admired Jeter growing up. Dan O'Dowd, the general manager of the Colorado Rockies, said one of the reasons he built his team around Tulowitzki was that he wanted a similar kind of leader.

"It's very difficult in this business, with 24 men around you, to have a player that can take other players to a higher level," O'Dowd said. "And Jeter does that in New York."

He has done it with sportsmanship and style, with a commanding presence and enduring decency, with signature moments that bridged ballparks and eras for the Yankees. He has done it, too, without letting us down, as a symbol of the game we yearn for baseball to be.

▲ Jeter stands in the batting cage during spring training in Tampa, Fla., *Feb. 24, 2006.*
Photo: Richard Perry, The New York Times

◄ Jeter and Bernie Williams, teammates from 1995 through 2006, share a moment in the dugout at Yankee Stadium, *June 26, 2005.*
Photo: Barton Silverman, The New York Times

"How many times are you going to say, 'What about that kid, Derek Jeter?'"

MANAGER JOE TORRE, *Sept. 22, 1996*

CHAPTER **1**

THE ROOKIE

He did not look the part. Shortstops could be flashy little guys like Ozzie Smith, or bigger guys with power like Cal Ripken Jr. But Derek Jeter? He was a reed. At 6 foot 3 and 180 pounds, he seemed too big to be a dynamo like Ozzie, and too frail to be a reliable hitter like Cal.

Yet Jeter possessed everything else: the drive to apply his extraordinary skills, the aptitude to do so quickly and the maturity to fit in seamlessly to a veteran team.

After the Yankees drafted him sixth overall in the 1992 draft, Jeter signed for $800,000 the day after his 18th birthday, forgoing a scholarship to the University of Michigan for the chance to join his favorite team.

In 1993, his first full professional season, he made 56 errors. The next year, he cut the errors by more than half, racing through three levels and dominating them all. His first major league season, in 1995, he hit .250 in 48 at-bats. His next season, his official rookie campaign, he was the unanimous American League Rookie of the Year and helped the Yankees win the World Series.

As Jeter floated down Broadway with his teammates, adoring girls proposed marriage. Jeter blushed. He was a champion and even a leader, all at age 22, with so much glory behind him, and yet so much still ahead.

Derek Jeter in 1995.
Photo: Diamond Images/ Getty Images

A Schoolboy Shortstop Gets a Bronx Invitation

June 2, 1992 | Derek Jeter has spent 12 summers visiting his grandparents in West Milford, N.J., and journeying to the Bronx to root for the Yankees. Today, Jeter moved closer to playing at Yankee Stadium someday because the Yankees selected the high school shortstop with the sixth overall pick in the amateur baseball draft.

Jeter was born in West Milford, moved to Kalamazoo, Mich., when he was 5, but his interest in the Yankees never dwindled and his baseball talents flourished.

Before injuring an ankle running over a slippery base in April, Jeter was considered a possible No. 1 choice overall because of his speed, arm strength and hitting. He wound up the first high school player chosen.

The Yankees must now begin the process of signing the 17-year-old. When they tabbed Brien Taylor as the No. 1 pick overall last season, the Yanks had acrimonious negotiations with the pitcher's adviser, Scott Boras, before finally signing Taylor to a record-setting $1.55 million deal.

With the draft rules changed so that a team now holds a high school player's rights for five years, it may be easier to sign draft picks. Jeter has accepted a baseball scholarship to Michigan. He completed high school with a 3.82 grade point average out of 4.0 and said today the odds were "50-50" on attending college or signing with the Yankees.

"We'll make a decision as a family," said Jeter, who hit .481 with 23 runs batted in for Kalamazoo Central High. "It is my dream to play professionally, whether it is now or after college."

As the sixth pick, Jeter could probably command a contract of close to $400,000. But Jeter downplayed monetary issues.

"I enjoy playing the game," said Jeter. "I think the money part is just an extra."

Jeter is the third shortstop the Yankees have selected first. Neither of the others, Dennis Sherrill (1974) and Rex Hudler (1978), ever became regular players.

The club released a statement about Jeter that simply said he was the best athlete available.

Jack Curry

In the Beginning, Even Jeter Doubted Jeter

June 18, 2007 | This was before the 2,242 hits, before he became the captain of the Yankees and before he attracted comparisons to Joe DiMaggio. This was Derek Jeter in Tampa, Fla., 15 years ago. This was Jeter's first day playing professionally for the Yankees.

Ricky Ledee was there starting for Class A Tampa, waiting to see the first-round draft choice who would immediately become the starting shortstop. Ledee's first impression of Jeter was that he was really skinny. Ledee held up his left pinky to show how thin he thought Jeter looked as an 18-year-old.

Jeter teased Ledee, his former minor league and major league teammate, behind the batting cage before the Yankees silenced the Mets, 8-2, at Yankee Stadium last night. Ledee is hanging on with the Mets, his seventh team.

Ledee smiled when he discussed the early days of watching a raw Jeter.

"He stunk," Ledee said. "In the beginning, he stunk."

Jeter acknowledged that, for a while, he did stink. In Jeter's debut, he went 0 for 7 with five strikeouts in a doubleheader and also made a throwing error that lost one of the games. Jeter, who had only one strikeout in 59 at-bats in his senior year in high school, was exasperated after several hours as a Yankee.

Jeter did not get a hit until his 15th at-bat. Ledee said Jeter's first hit was a bloop single to right field.

Ledee said Jeter was so flummoxed as a hitter that simply putting the ball in play was an accomplishment. Was this the talented player from Kalamazoo, Mich., the Yankees gave an $800,000 signing bonus?

The first time Jeter met his teammates at a Gulf Coast League game, he was driven there by a Yankees executive. Ledee, who had taken the one-hour bus ride with the team, said some players grumbled about how the new player had received preferential treatment. Ledee said they were moaning even more once Jeter actually played a day later.

Statistically, Jeter did struggle with his first minor league team. He hit .202 with 3 homers, 25 runs batted in and 12 errors in 47 games.

But while Jeter looked overwhelmed, Ledee said the skinny prospect had skills.

"You could see that everything was there," Ledee said. "The bat speed was there. He stayed inside the ball and hit the ball the other way. The Jeter that I see now, he was the same then."

No matter how much Jeter struggled, Ledee said he stayed focused.

"You don't know if, in his room, he was fighting himself," Ledee said. "But, on the field, you never saw that."

"Back in the hotel, I might have gotten down," Jeter said. "But not in front of anybody."

Jack Curry

Jeter works out at Yankee Stadium.
Photo: Diamond Images/ Getty Images

Jeter Is Moving Up Quickly

Aug. 26, 1994 | Derek Jeter is a former first-round draft pick who has catapulted from Class A to Class AAA in two months. Manager Buck Showalter of the Yankees studied Jeter for five games last week. He analyzed Jeter in the dugout and the clubhouse and watched how he interacted with teammates on a club that has two shortstops with big league experience.

The manager liked what he observed. "Those are things I want to see," he said, lauding Jeter's quickness and fearlessness. "Those are things you can't get in a report."

Stump Merrill has managed Jeter for 25 games at Columbus, where the 6-foot-3-inch, 180-pounder, who wiggles his bat and has the hip-hop swagger of the basketball player he used to be, has batted .314 with 2 homers, 13 runs batted in, 7 steals and 5 errors.

When asked what has most impressed him, Merrill said, "Everything."

When asked what he needs to improve upon, Jeter replied, "Everything."

Although he declined to handicap Jeter's chances of reaching the Yankees next season, General Manager Gene Michael, a former shortstop, said: "He's the real thing. I liked what I saw of him. He's getting there."

Jeter does not believe the hype, or at least he does not let himself believe it. He hit .329 in 69 games at Class A Fort Lauderdale, then was bumped to Class AA Albany, where he hit .377 in 34 games. On Aug. 1, he found himself peeking at the majors from Columbus.

Obviously, his glove will determine whether he is Showalter's shortstop in 1995. If Showalter is comfortable with Jeter's defense, where his shortcomings have been a tendency to throw every ball to first at warp speed and to botch the routine play, he could appear in the Bronx.

Jack Curry

▲ Baseball America's minor league player of the year poses on the dugout steps at Yankee Stadium, *Sept. 14, 1994.*
Photo: Mark Lennihan, Associated Press

► Jeter shows his defensive prowess, completing a double play while avoiding Jim Vatcher of the Norfolk Tides, the New York Mets' AAA team, at Harbor Park, Norfolk, Va., *Aug. 17, 1994.*
Photo: Paul Aiken, The Virginian-Pilot

"I don't know what's going to happen. But I always knew the Yankees don't move people too quickly, so I was a little surprised when I came here."

DEREK JETER on advancing from Class A to Class AAA in two months, *Aug. 26, 1994*

Jeter hits the ball during one of his 15 games as a Yankee in 1995, when he had 12 hits in 48 at-bats — an inauspicious debut before his impressive 1996 rookie season.

Photo: Focus on Sport/Getty Images

"If he hits .240 or thereabouts and plays solid defense, he'll be fine."

JOE TORRE, *March 12, 1996*

Humbling Start for Jeter in '95 Debut

Sept. 9, 2009 | Derek Jeter's first major league game ended with an 0-for-5 performance at the plate and a postgame meal at McDonald's. Fourteen years and 2,718 hits ago, the most memorable part of Jeter's night might have been the inexpensive hamburgers he shared with his dad.

The sterile Kingdome in Seattle was the setting for Jeter's debut on May 29, 1995, which included his striking out with the go-ahead run on third base in the 11th inning. (The Yankees lost, 8-7, in 12 innings.)

After Jeter's drab opening, he and his father, Charles, trudged past a series of darkened restaurants before spotting the most familiar of fast-food spots.

"It was the only place that was open," said Jeter, who paused and added, "I treated."

But in late May 1995, Jeter was a 20-year-old looking for his first hit. It came the next night, in Jeter's seventh at-bat in the majors, when he slapped a single between shortstop and third base off the Mariners' Tim Belcher.

"I could pull it back then," Jeter joked Monday.

The ball was removed from the game so Jeter would have it as a memento. The date was inscribed on the ball, May 30, 1995, and it sits in Jeter's parents' house in New Jersey.

The only reason Jeter was even in position to collect that first hit was because Tony Fernandez, the starting Yankees shortstop, had strained a rib-cage muscle. Although Jeter was hitting .354 at Class AAA Columbus, the Yankees initially promoted Robert Eenhoorn, a steady defensive infielder.

In Eenhoorn's first three games, he was 0 for 7. That ended his audition, and the Yankees summoned Jeter. When Jeter called home, he waited until his father was on the telephone, then yelled, "I'm out of here!" — his emphatic way of saying that he was headed to the majors.

"The weird thing with him was, although he was taking your job, you were still pulling for him," Eenhoorn said of Jeter. "He was such a nice guy."

In Jeter's second game, he ended up with two hits off Belcher.

Jeter's first stint with the Yankees ended after 13 games. The Yankees briefly considered switching Fernandez to second base so Jeter could stay at shortstop, but they decided against it. Before Jeter traveled to Class AAA, Don Mattingly told him, "You'll be back."

He returned for two games in September, and by the next season, Jeter was the Yankees' shortstop. His hit-o-meter has churned consistently ever since.

Jack Curry

Torre Is Sure of Only One Thing: Jeter Is His Shortstop

Dec. 13, 1995 | Joe Torre still does not know whether David Cone will pitch on opening day for the Yankees, but the new manager revealed yesterday that Derek Jeter will play shortstop. The hype that has followed Jeter throughout a marvelous minor league career will finally be transferred to the Bronx on a full-time basis.

"The organization feels it's his time to play," said Torre, who has never seen Jeter play in person. "We're going to be patient with him and see how it develops. But Tony Fernandez hopefully will be there in the event we need him to back up for us."

The 21-year-old Jeter, who has not met Torre and who did not know the Yankees had elevated him on the depth chart until alerted by a reporter, does not expect to fumble his chance.

"Oh, yeah, I'm going to be ready to earn the job," Jeter said. "I'm going to spring training ready. It's not something I'm going to let pass by."

Jeter, the 1992 first-round draft pick, hit .317 with 2 homers, 45 runs batted in, 20 steals and 29 errors for Class AAA Columbus last year. In two stints with the Yankees, he batted .250 with 7 r.b.i. in 15 games. The 33-year-old Fernandez, who is in the final year of a two-year, $3 million contract, hit a disappointing .245 and endured various injuries last season.

"Derek Jeter is going to be our shortstop going in," said Torre, who did not sound overly thrilled about a rookie anchoring the infield. "We may have to suffer through some growing pains early on, but that's our plan."

"It's a good feeling knowing you have the opportunity," Jeter said. "No one is going to hand you the job."

Jack Curry

Jeter swings in his
first at-bat on opening
day — with his first major
league home run coming
in his next time up
against the Indians in
Cleveland, *April 2, 1996.*
Photo: Carl Skalak for
The New York Times

New York Shortstops Inspire Sweepstakes

April 3, 1996 | After watching Rey Ordonez break into 1996 in a most spectacular way, the great shortstop Ozzie Smith declared that the young Mets emigre from Cuba is the second coming of himself.

Well, after Yankee fans watched their own highly touted rookie shortstop, Derek Jeter, make his debut against the Cleveland Indians yesterday, who could fault them if they asked the Wizard to make room for a third?

Jeter not only gave Yankee fans reason to recall Tom Tresh, the last rookie to start at short for the Yankees, in 1962, but he also became the first Yankee rookie to hit an opening-day home run since Jerry Kenney in 1969. He also made an immediate impression with the glove to help preserve David Cone's 7-1 victory in Cleveland.

Thus did Jeter refuse to be outdone in the nascent but potentially riveting battle extraordinaire between two of the most celebrated young shortstops to hit New York in a long, long time.

"He played outstanding defensively," Manager Joe Torre beamed. "He did everything today."

Ordonez has come packaged as the Glove, while the rangy Jeter, built more like Cal Ripken than Ozzie Smith, could rightfully be called the Bat because of his .306 minor league batting average and a boatload of minor league player of the year trophies.

So it was not that surprising when Jeter in some way solved the Indians' veteran, Dennis Martinez, in the fifth inning when he hit a 2-0 pitch into the left-field seats to give the Yankees a 2-0 lead.

The question has always been Jeter's glove. He shut down the inquiries for today. In the second inning, Jeter ranged far to his right to make a backhanded snare of a Sandy Alomar grounder in the hole for the out. Granted, he didn't throw Alomar out from his knees, as Ordonez did a Cardinals runner at home from the left-field line well behind third base Monday, but the play was first-rate.

Then in the seventh, Jeter contributed the pivotal defensive play of the game.

Cone was nursing a two-run lead in the seventh when Alomar hit a two-out double. Omar Vizquel then flicked a Cone pitch in the air toward no-man's land in shallow center. The first thought was that not even Bernie Williams could track down the dying quail. But Yankees' panic turned into glee as Jeter ranged out to make an over-the-shoulder running one-handed catch.

"It was hit kind of high, so I thought I had a pretty good chance to get to it," Jeter said matter-of-factly. Williams, a little more animated, recalled thinking: "al-righhht, because I was not going to get that ball."

The early scouting reports on Jeter suggested that Williams should have been surprised. Not so, Williams said, "because I've seen him make that catch several times this spring."

Playing for his family — his mother here and in Michigan his father and little sister, Sharlee, who is a high school shortstop — Jeter succeeded in doing what Torre hoped and he desired. He showed that he is more than a hitter clogging up the middle. "Don't get me wrong, I enjoyed the home run, but playing defense comes first."

Claire Smith

Jeter Quietly Goes About Business

April 7, 1996 | You are 21 years old and starting at shortstop for the Yankees. You are already being mentioned as a Rookie of the Year candidate and you have been the most impressive player on the field when it has not been drenched. You are creeping toward the stardom that has been forecast since 1992. You could behave like a star or you could continue behaving like your modest self. Derek Jeter behaves like himself and that is refreshing. Very refreshing.

The hundreds of lectures and lessons that Charles and Dorothy Jeter provided ever since Derek boldly announced that he planned to be a baseball player have obviously sunk in.

Jeter listened and responded to what his parents preached about realizing expectations in athletics and academics, handling responsibilities and being humble. His actions speak for him. Do not expect his words to do the same. Ever.

"In our house, you couldn't go around talking about yourself," said Jeter, shaking his head to emphasize the point. "I really don't like people who talk about themselves a lot. It's all right to have confidence, but without the cockiness. I don't talk too much about myself."

But others do and will as the former first-round draft pick blossoms in his rookie year. He stole some of the spotlight from David Cone on opening day in Cleveland by smashing his first major league homer and with a wondrous over-the-shoulder catch to protect a 2-0 lead.

Jeter looked even smoother with three hits and three runs scored to spark a 5-1 decision over the American League champions the next night. But Jeter is so grounded that he shrewdly switched the focus to the team when quizzed about his immediate exploits.

"Winning has been the best thing for me," Jeter said. "Especially when you get to this level. That's what it's all about. Everybody wants to win. You want to get to the postseason. Last year, I got a chance to see what that was like. I want to get back there."

Still, beneath the careful answers lurks a poised player with a touch of brashness that he does not display. Before finishing Little League, Jeter told his father he would be the shortstop for the Yankees.

"When he gets on the field, he's extremely confident," Charles Jeter said. "It's not something he's going to talk about, but I know it's there."

"I've been waiting for this my whole life," Derek Jeter said. "I think I'm ready."

Somehow, it does not sound boastful when Jeter utters it. Not when he has called his 16-year-old sister, Sharlee, the superior shortstop.

Not when he chides himself for completing only one semester toward a degree at Michigan because he has been so immersed in baseball during the off-season.

"At this rate, I'm looking at graduating in 2020," Jeter said. "You have until your junior year to pick a major. That gives me a good 15 or 20 years."

Before Manager Joe Torre's debut with the Yankees, which was also Jeter's debut as the full-time shortstop, the rookie strolled past the veteran who had been in pro baseball since 1960 and asked, "Are you ready?" Torre was pleasantly stunned.

"Being a middle infielder, I know defense comes first," Jeter said. "But I want to hit, too. I'm not going to be happy if I hit .240."

gain, it sounds more factual than boastful. One snippet of Jeter's life helps indicate why he is not pretentious. His parents trekked over four hours from Kalamazoo, Mich., to Cleveland on Monday to watch opening day, but it was snowed out.

His mother returned for the games on Tuesday and Wednesday, but his father stayed home to attend Sharlee's softball opener for Kalamazoo Central High School.

"She's just as important as I am," Jeter said. "My parents equally divide it. She's the best player, too, so they wanted to see her. Why would they want to only see me?"

You are Derek Jeter. You will live in Manhattan and do not expect to be overwhelmed because you will remain reserved and because there are several relatives in New Jersey to dispense advice. You will not change because you cannot.

"If I ever want to go home, I can't change," Jeter said. "I've got to keep the same mentality and be the same person. Baseball can humble you quick. You can have a good week and then have a terrible two weeks. You have to keep an even keel."

Jack Curry

Jeter Delivers a 4-for-4 Sparkler

July 3, 1996 | Derek Jeter backed out of the batter's box, shaking his head over and over while staring at Brian O'Nora, the plate umpire. As if there was not enough pressure on the Yankee shortstop after the Boston Red Sox intentionally walked Jim Leyritz to load the bases in the tie game, Jeter now had to contend with a pitch he thought should have made the count 3-0. Instead, it was called a strike. The rookie simmered.

But he coolly slapped Joe Hudson's next pitch between shortstop and third to score two runs, break a 5-5 tie in the seventh inning and help the Yankees to a 7-5 victory at Yankee Stadium last night.

Once Jeter rounded first base, he had forgotten the call and was celebrating the first four-hit game of his career. Jeter's first three singles did not figure in the scoring, but his final single off Hudson was crucial.

"He's taken on a lot of responsibility," Manager Joe Torre said. "As long as he keeps working hard, I'm not sure what his limit is."

"To me, this is still just a game," Jeter said. "I'm having fun. You can't do well unless you're having fun. I don't think about the pressure of the situation."

Jack Curry

Questions for a Rookie Shortstop

Aug. 11, 1996 | **Why were you attracted to playing shortstop?** My dad played short in college. When you're young, you want to be like your dad.

What makes a solid shortstop? You have to be someone who's not afraid to take control. I don't think you can be timid.

What is it like to play shortstop in New York, where there is constant scrutiny and pressure? I wouldn't trade it for anything. In New York, you can do pretty much whatever you want to do. It's the city that never sleeps.

Why have you been able to feel so comfortable as a rookie? Any time anyone doubts me, I try to work that much harder to prove them wrong. I like to try to prove people wrong.

If a teammate has a no-hitter with two outs in the ninth inning, who do you want the last ball hit to? Me. That way you're always linked with it. Every time they show highlights of the no-hitter, you're always there. That's cool.

What is the most comfortable place in the world for you? I'm most comfortable on the field. It's something I've done my whole life.

Do you think about winning Rookie of the Year? You can't help but think about it because people talk about it. But I'd much rather win a World Series in my first year.

If someone told you tomorrow that you could never play another inning at shortstop, how would you feel? The first thing I would do is finish college.

Jack Curry

Jeter's Poise

Sept. 18, 1996 | Jeter, the leading candidate for Rookie of the Year, carries himself like old-style Yankees who came down the Bronx Pike every so often — Tony Kubek, Bobby Richardson and Willie Randolph.

Jeter has been solid on defense and at bat, playing 146 games and batting .316 and holding his errors to 19. The other day, Joe Torre was asked if he had ever seen a young player as poised as Jeter. Torre gave a long pause and then said: "The only player I would compare him to is Ripken, the way Cal was with the Orioles in 1983. He is poised in a very key position. You don't see many kids like him."

When he heard what the manager had said, Jeter said politely: "I think it's an insult to Cal Ripken to compare him to me. But that's very nice of Mr. Torre to say so."

George Vecsey

Jeter Made Difference for Yankees

Sept. 26, 1996 | As the Yankees clinched the American League East last night, the kid at shortstop has been the difference in their season. For all the potential he has fulfilled with his .320 average and silky smooth glove, back on opening day the Yankees weren't sure what to expect from him.

When the games mean more, some young players find it a lot harder to play. But this rookie hasn't.

"When we opened the season, yes, there was some concern about him; he was overcharging balls," recalled Don Zimmer, the Yankee bench coach who was once a shortstop. "Now he's going to be the Rookie of the Year in our league, but it's like he ain't a rookie. And he's going to get better."

The last Yankee shortstop to be the A.L. Rookie of the Year was Tom Tresh in 1962, with a .286 average. In the years before there was an official rookie award, Phil Rizzuto hit .307 in 1941.

"I just like it when a young player comes into the big leagues the way Derek has," said Willie Randolph, the third-base coach. "You believe in yourself and you carry that talent with respect for the veterans and the game. He still gets a little careless in the field, but as a hitter, he has no fear."

To appreciate the difference Jeter has made in the Yankees, consider what they would have done had he flopped. Tony Fernandez was unavailable, out with a damaged elbow. Mariano Duncan could have played shortstop, but who would have played second?

Instead, in starting 153 of 158 games, Jeter's future is now, after five different shortstops were in the opening-day lineup the five previous seasons: Fernandez, Mike Gallego, Spike Owen, Randy Velarde and Alvaro Espinosa.

Jeter doesn't scare. On a double play, some shortstops want their second baseman to throw them the ball at, say, shoulder level.

"But when I asked Derek where exactly he wanted the ball on a double play," Duncan said, "he told me, 'Any place you throw it, I'll get it.' And he has. He plays the game so nice and easy and relaxed, he don't even look like a rookie."

Late in last week's twilight-night doubleheader with the Orioles, Chris Chambliss, the batting coach, turned to Randolph and said, "Look at Jeter, he's not even tired." And as the difference for the Yankees, he knows he's just begun to play.

"Derek wants to play every day," Joe Torre said with a laugh. "When I rested him a few months ago, he told me, 'How am I going to catch Cal Ripken?'"

Dave Anderson

Ruben Rivera, left, congratulates Bernie Williams for his ninth-inning grand slam against the Tigers in Detroit. Jeter, behind Williams, and Joe Girardi also scored, *Sept. 12, 1996. Photo: Blake J. Discher for The New York Times*

Jeter's the Real Thing

Sept. 29, 1996 | I returned to Yankee Stadium for the first game of three against the second-place Baltimore Orioles, the series that would more or less settle the pennant race. The omens were in our favor, and I could reflect on some specific and genuine fanly pleasures.

Most of all I reveled in Derek Jeter, who seems a character out of a storybook. A hero for the 90's. A shortstop, just 21, he's handsome, unflappable, graceful. And this year he has emerged as a star, almost supernaturally composed in the pennant race frying pan; I know he's the real thing because I've committed his body language to memory, intrigued particularly by the way he watches pitches pass outside, leaning over the plate to judge if it will graze the outside corner or miss it, rising up on his toes and needing to catch his balance so as not to tip over after the ball goes by. I can recognize his walk from behind, the way I used to be able to do with Maris, Mantle, Munson, Mattingly.

Bruce Weber

Torre Relies on Veterans, and Jeter, Too

Oct. 3, 1996 | Derek Jeter, the rookie who led the veterans for much of the season, reversed his postseason troubles to help the Yankees win Game 2 of the opening-round playoff series, 5-4, in 12 grueling innings last night at Yankee Stadium.

Jeter ended a three-hit night with a single to lead off the final inning, then scored after a walk and a throwing error by Texas Rangers third baseman Dean Palmer.

Joe Torre, so prescient about his players, addressed Jeter's Game 1 performance, in which the shortstop went 1 for 4 and stranded runner after runner, by saying before the second game: "The difference about the postseason is that you still want to lean on experienced guys. To me, Jeter is different. I've been around a lot of young kids and a lot of rookies. He's done a lot of growing up this year. He doesn't see the postseason as something different."

Claire Smith

Jeter, right, and
Tim Raines get tangled
up with a fan falling onto
the field while they all
try for a pop foul ball
during a game against
the Texas Rangers in
Arlington, *Oct. 5, 1996.*
Photo: G. Paul Burnett,
The New York Times

◀ Jeff Maier, 12, deflects Jeter's fly ball away from Orioles right fielder Tony Tarasco and into the stands at Yankee Stadium, *Oct. 9, 1996. Photo: Mark Lennihan, Associated Press*

▼ Teammates greet No. 2 after his controversial home run. *Photo: G. Paul Burnett, The New York Times*

Winning with a Boy's Help, the Yankees Make No Apologies

Oct. 10, 1996 | One overzealous 12-year-old helped the Yankees rejoice on a day when all of their runs except Bernie Williams's game-winning homer were somewhat tainted. Still, after beating the Baltimore Orioles, 5-4, in 11 innings yesterday, the Yankees refused to apologize.

They won their first American League Championship Series game in 15 years, and did it with an assist from 12-year-old Jeff Maier, a New Jersey boy with a keen eye and a quick glove. The young fan lived out every kid's dream, bringing his mitt to Yankee Stadium and getting a chance to use it. In the bottom of the eighth inning, Maier reached over the wall in right field to scoop a ball hit by New York's Derek Jeter away from Baltimore's right fielder and into the stands.

The Orioles screamed for interference, but it was ruled a home run. Although the umpire later second-guessed his call, the home run stood, the Yankees had tied the score at 4-4 and were on their way to a dramatic Game 1 victory.

Jeter wants to meet the boy to thank him and "Good Morning America" telephoned his house in Old Tappan, N.J., minutes after the game to try to schedule him on the show. The Orioles, who were rightfully perturbed, saw the incident as another indignity at the hands of a team that has now beaten them 11 out of 14 times this year.

Leading off the bottom of the 11th, Williams rocked Randy Myers's 1-1 slider deep into the left-field seats. It was his fourth home run this October, and it vaulted the Yankees to their fourth straight come-from-behind triumph in the postseason. The Yankees were delirious, and Jeff Maier was delighted.

"It's unbelievable," Jeff said. "It's pretty cool."

"Do I feel bad?" asked Jeter. "We won the game. Why should I feel bad? Ask them that."

It came when the Yankees needed it most, trailing by a run. Jeter hit a towering fly ball to right off Armando Benitez that Tony Tarasco positioned himself to snare by backing up against the fence. Tarasco was waiting for the ball to descend into his glove when Maier dipped his glove down about two feet and scooped the ball over the fence as it glanced off his arm. Umpire Rich Garcia signaled for a homer and Tarasco and the Orioles fumed.

Television replays clearly showed that without interference, the ball would have hit near the top of the fence or Tarasco would have caught it to put the Orioles four outs away from a 4-3 victory. But Maier was stationed in the walkway in front of the first row and, as kids sometimes do, he got in the way. The Yankees are fortunate he did.

"It was like a magic trick," explained Tarasco. "I was getting ready to catch it and suddenly a glove appeared and the ball disappeared. When the kid reached over the wall, the kid's glove was very close to mine."

Garcia, who did not think Maier interfered with Tarasco, said he thought the ball was leaving the Stadium and that the right fielder did not have a chance to snare it. After watching the replay, he was asked if he still thought Jeter deserved a homer.

"Well, after looking at it, no," he said. "At the time I saw it, I never saw anybody touch the ball and I thought the ball was out of the ballpark."

Jeter rationalized that he would have been awarded at least a double anyway and, since Tim Raines belted the next pitch for a single off Benitez, the score would have been eventually tied, 4-4, even if Maier did not get involved.

Jack Curry

Jeter autographs base-
balls for young fans be-
fore Game 5 of the World
Series against
the Atlanta Braves at
Fulton County Stadium,
Oct. 24, 1996.
Photo: Stephen Dunn,
Getty Images

A Return to Glory

Oct. 27, 1996 | From every poignant moment to every marvelous play to every memorable rally, the Yankees' season unfolded like some unbelievable baseball fairy tale. Again and again, the Yankees outdid themselves in inspiration and in achievement, and last night at Yankee Stadium the Yankees provided a joyous conclusion to their special story.

The Yankees stopped the Atlanta Braves, 3-2, in Game 6 to win the World Series and make one of New York's most unforgettable teams even more noteworthy. The Yankees overcame a 2-0 deficit in the series with four straight stylish victories against the defending champions. So, the best team in baseball resides in the Bronx for the first time since the Yankees won the World Series in 1978, and will be toasted with a parade on Tuesday morning.

Bernie Williams and Derek Jeter, their twin Mr. Octobers, and Joe Girardi, who made a late cameo appearance, each drove in a run off Greg Maddux in a three-run third that supplied enough offense. Maddux and the Braves looked mortal, and the Yankees looked special.

Jack Curry

"We played hooky to see our rookie."

A HANDMADE SIGN HELD UP BY A TEEN-AGE GIRL, with no need
to mention the name Derek Jeter, *Oct. 30, 1996*

"His eyes, his lips. The way he bats."

A TEEN-AGE GIRL FROM QUEENS on why Jeter is "so fine," *Oct. 30, 1996*

Adoration, Adulation and Even
Some Marriage Proposals

Oct. 30, 1996 | Kenny Rogers sat atop the sparkling blue-and-white parade float, waving a gigantic Yankee flag. David Cone stood on the edge of the same float and pointed and clapped in appreciation. Derek Jeter blushed as wailing teen-age girls treated him like a rock star and held up placards with marriage proposals.

The Yankees were enveloped by endless streams of confetti, toilet paper, blank credit card receipts and by endless adulation, adoration and attention as their 60-vehicle convoy cruised through lower Manhattan for their ticker-tape celebration. It was difficult to detect whether the World Series champion Yankees or their maniacal fans were more elated. Call it mutual elation on this day of celebration.

Derek Jeter, *May 2004.*
Photo: Ronald C. Modra, Getty Images

It's No Contest as Jeter Captures Rookie of the Year

Nov. 5, 1996 | Derek Jeter was supposed to be the question mark on the Yankees this season, even according to Manager Joe Torre. Could the rookie handle playing shortstop? Could he succeed in New York? What would happen to the Yankees if the youngster floundered?

Imagine how ludicrous those concerns seem now.

Jeter's stylish play forced those questions to vanish faster than World Series tickets. The only question Jeter had to answer yesterday was where he planned to display his newest trophy, the American League Rookie of the Year award he won in a landslide.

The 22-year-old Jeter garnered all 28 first-place votes in becoming the fifth American Leaguer since the award's inception 50 years ago to be a unanimous choice for the honor.

No one was surprised. Not even the normally humble Jeter.

After Jeter homered off Cleveland's Dennis Martinez and made a nifty over-the-shoulder catch in the Yankees' season opener, he immediately became a strong candidate for the award. When the glorious season progressed and Jeter became a special and instrumental part of the Yankees' magical ride, it became more obvious that he would be named the premier rookie.

"I'm still dreaming," Jeter said yesterday. "The way New York has embraced us after the championship, I can't put it into words. This is still a dream. I hope we can do it a few more years."

Jeter was the first Yankee to win the award since Dave Righetti in 1981, the second-youngest Yankee to be voted the award after Tony Kubek (21 years old in 1957) and the eighth Yankee over all. He easily outdistanced the Chicago White Sox right-hander James Baldwin.

California's Tim Salmon was the last rookie to win unanimously in the American League, in 1993.

"Unanimous?" joked Jeter. "I must have had some of my family voting in it."

Not really. With 5 points for a first-place vote, 3 for second and 1 for third in the voting by two news media members from each American League city, Jeter secured 140 points. Baldwin notched 64 points, Detroit's Tony Clark had 30 and Baltimore's Rocky Coppinger and Kansas City's Jose Rosado tied for fourth with 6 points.

t was another wondrous day for Jeter, who hugged his father, Charles, during a news conference at Yankee Stadium and thanked "Mr. Steinbrenner" and "Mr. Torre" for having patience with him. Jeter even suggested that the Yankees could have demoted him to the minor leagues after he had an uneventful spring, but that was never a consideration. The Yankees wanted him to learn on the job and he did. Quickly and emphatically.

"We had a lot of guys who were valuable," said Torre. "I don't think we had one guy, player-wise, who was more valuable than him."

Torre said last February that he hoped Jeter would bat .240 and play dependable defense. The rookie exceeded those goals by hitting .314 — the highest among the 10 shortstops voted rookies of the year — with 10 homers, 78 runs batted in, 104 runs scored and 22 errors in 157 games.

He evolved into perhaps the Yankees' premier player following the All-Star Game break, batting .350 with 6 homers and 40 r.b.i. to finish the regular season with a flourish, clinch the rookie award and secure a $10,000 contractual bonus.

Though the rookie voting is completed when the regular season ends, Jeter was even more impressive in the pressure-packed October as veterans like Wade Boggs, Paul O'Neill and Tino Martinez struggled for the Yankees. Jeter had a

.361 average in the postseason — including one unforgettable homer against Baltimore that was helped by an overzealous 12-year-old — with 3 r.b.i. and 12 runs scored. Jeter helped usher the Yankees to their first World Series title since 1978, never looking like a player who would be a college senior right now.

"It's tremendous," said Charles Jeter. "Derek is doing what he wants to do. I'm most proud of the way he carries himself beyond the baseball end. As a parent, I'm proud of the way he handled himself."

When Jeter was asked what would inspire him in 1997 after a grandiose debut, he responded: "To come back. It was incredible. The parade. How the city took to us. I want to be back year after year. There's nothing else I'd rather do than win some more."

Jack Curry

Derek Jeter has practically
patented his jump throw, this
time trying (unsuccessfully)
to beat Chris Woodward of
the Seattle Mariners to first
base at Yankee Stadium,
June 30, 2009.
Photo: Barton Silverman,
The New York Times

"Jeter can do everything. He's polished. He can inside-out balls. He can turn on balls, drive them. In today's game, he's your typical 2-hitter. He can play hit-and-run, has a good eye, has good bat control."

TONY GWYNN of the San Diego Padres, during the World Series, *Oct. 20, 1998*

CHAPTER ❷

THE ATHLETE

The prototypical five-tool player can hit for average, hit for power, run, throw and field. Derek Jeter has it all in his toolbox, a package of skills that, taken together, encompasses so many of the acts that make baseball beautiful.

Ever since his amateur days, Jeter has had the uncanny ability to take an inside pitch and drive it to right field for a single. But he also has power that way, and sometimes it can be extraordinary: Jeter has surprised himself by smashing upper-deck home runs to right.

He is a master of small-ball arts, bunting much more often than the average superstar and stealing bases when the strategy dictates. He shows his arm strength with his signature defensive move, the jump throw across the diamond from deep in the hole between shortstop and third.

Because that play makes such a dazzling highlight, statistical analysts have often argued that Jeter's defense is overrated.

But the managers and coaches who select Gold Glove winners have honored him repeatedly, and Jeter has produced at least two unforgettable defensive moments: his flip to the plate in a 2001 playoff game at Oakland, and his dive into the stands catching a critical fly ball against Boston in 2004.

Jeter's father played shortstop at Fisk University, so the position is in the family blood, and Jeter seems to have no intention of ever leaving. The young shortstops who broke into the majors with him — Nomar Garciaparra, Alex Rodriguez and others — have retired or changed positions, while Jeter rolls on.

Before He Played Shortstop

March 29, 1998 | The Yankees' shortstop spent a year playing second. "In Little League," Derek Jeter said.

He was 11 years old and his coach inserted Jeter's best friend, Josh Ewbank, at shortstop and played Jeter at second. Jeter did not care for this, but his coach told him to stop worrying about things he could not control and just enjoy himself. His coach was named Charles Jeter.

Derek Jeter wanted to play shortstop because his father played shortstop, for Fisk University in Nashville. Derek watched his father play softball and was struck by how much fun his father seemed to have. Years later, Jeter would say his father's greatest contribution to his own game is a love for baseball.

When Jeter was 15, he played third base for Rathco, a summer league team sponsored by a company that produces highway safety equipment, road barriers and such. The next season he joined the Kalamazoo Maroons. He already was tall, 6 feet 1 or 6 feet 2, and very skinny, said Dan Hinga, the Maroons' coach. The team played games almost daily, with little time for practice. Michigan's cold climate tightly frames the baseball season, and it was as if Jeter tried to cram a year's worth of baseball into a few months. He would arrive early for games and take grounders. "And after games," Hinga said, "he would stand out there and take grounders as long as there was somebody there to hit balls to him. People say Derek is lucky. Well, Derek is fortunate that he's 6-3 and he's got long arms and legs. But he worked his rear end off."

Jeter had a powerful arm even as a teen-ager. Watching his unusual mechanics — Jeter throws with his chest puffed out, like a quarterback — Hinga figured out that Jeter grew up flinging baseballs as far as he could, as part of his normal warm-up routine, building his arm strength and developing the muscles in his upper torso. Most players warm up throwing 60 to 90 feet, Hinga said. Jeter threw much, much farther.

Jeter moved to shortstop for good at 16, making spectacular plays and sometimes fumbling routine grounders. But Hinga knew he would be a special player. Playing a game in Battle Creek, Jeter, thin as he was, smashed two homers in one game out of cavernous Nichols Field, blasts of 400 feet or more. Hinga saw this and peered into the future.

Buster Olney

"Gliding runner w/ burst-type acceleration. . . . very qk. feet, very gd. lower body control. Arm strength to spare! Excellent carry and can throw from all angles."

CHUCK MCMICHAEL of the Kansas City Royals

"Slender, agile body with long arms and legs. Large feet. . . . Outstanding infield instincts. Soft hands and strong, accurate arm. Bat has quickness. . . . Makes contact with gap power. Will hit occasional long ball. Comes to play."

TONY STEIL of the Atlanta Braves

EXCERPTS FROM 1992 SCOUTING REPORTS on Derek Jeter, then a 17-year-old high school shortstop, *May 9, 1999*

Jeter reels backward from a high and tight pitch in a home game against the Texas Rangers, *Sept. 30, 1998.* *Photo: Ozier Muhammad, The New York Times*

Jeter Makes an Adjustment in His Swing

March 16, 1998 | Believe it or not, there has been more to Derek Jeter's spring training than contract talks and dinner with Mariah Carey. Teen-age girls who coo his name each time he comes to bat may not care, but he has made a major alteration to his swing, and he is driving the ball more.

Jeter is having a staggering spring at the plate, hitting .381 with a .714 slugging percentage, and Manager Joe Torre said today in Tampa, Fla., that Jeter would bat second, after the leadoff hitter, Chuck Knoblauch.

The right-handed-hitting Jeter came to the big leagues two years ago possessing the ability to hit an inside pitch to right field, an unusual talent for a young player. He could extend his arms on pitches outside and drive the ball. But opposing pitchers — especially the Seattle staff — began to hammer fastballs inside to him repeatedly, rarely giving him a chance to extend his arms. Last year, Jeter batted only .149 against the Mariners.

Jeter determined that he would learn how to drive an inside pitch to left field; when pitchers throw inside fastballs, he wants to be able to extend his arms and pull the ball.

Living in Tampa during the off-season, Jeter worked daily with a batting tee, under the tutelage of Gary Denbo, the organization's hitting coordinator.

He corrected a habit of leaning forward as he swung. Using the tee, he has forced himself to keep his upper body more erect. When he sees an inside fastball now, he often whips the bat around and drives the ball.

Torre believes the apparent improvement is due, in large measure, to experience. Torre recalled that when he first saw Henry Aaron in the major leagues, Aaron almost always hit the ball to right field. As Aaron learned about pitchers, about pitch recognition and about what pitches to expect in certain ball-strike counts, he began to drive the ball more, all over the field. Jeter, Torre believes, is learning about all this now, learning how to anticipate situations when pitchers must throw meaty fastballs and how to take advantage of them.

According to the conventional wisdom, Jeter will get more fastballs to hit this year because he will be batting behind Knoblauch. Last year, Knoblauch reached base 279 times and stole 62 bases. If he has a similar season in 1998, Jeter will continually bat in situations when Knoblauch will be a threat to steal.

Opposing catchers will want to give themselves the best possible chance to throw out Knoblauch and will be less likely to call for changeups and breaking balls, pitches that are harder to catch. They will be far more likely to call for fastballs, and Jeter, older and smarter, stronger from hours of weight lifting, should be able to take advantage.

Jeter had 48 extra-base hits last year, including 10 home runs. "He's got the strength to hit 20 home runs," said Mark Newman, the club's vice president for player development.

Hitting home runs may be the only skill that separates Jeter and Nomar Garciaparra, the Boston infielder.

Buster Olney

At Shortstop, 3 Leaders of the Pack

May 22, 1998 | The Yankees' Phil Rizzuto had to wait 38 years before his induction into baseball's Hall of Fame certified the golden age of shortstops that he, Pee Wee Reese and Alvin Dark created in New York City in the 1940's and 1950's.

No one should wait that long to conclude that there is a renaissance under way in the middle infield.

Derek Jeter. Alex Rodriguez. Nomar Garciaparra. The shortstops for the Yankees, the Seattle Mariners and the Boston Red Sox, respectively, are the crown princes gracing the position today.

Their galaxy also includes several others: the Expos' under-appreciated Mark Grudzielanek; the Blue Jays' undiscovered Alex Gonzalez; the Mets' Rey Ordonez; the Indians' Omar Vizquel; the Cardinals' Royce Clayton and the Marlins' Edgar Renteria.

"If you really sat down and started naming all the shortstops, there's a certain excitement over that position that hasn't been there in a while," said the Baltimore Orioles' Cal Ripken Jr., who redefined the position in the 1980's as one associated with offense as well as defense.

Ripken, now playing third base, sees his successors continue to redefine the position with even smoother blends of defense and batting prowess. No one has caught his eye, or that of anyone else, more than Jeter, Rodriguez and Garciaparra.

"They are fabulously talented," Ripken said. "It's exciting to watch them develop. It's one of the great things about baseball to watch someone come to the big leagues with some raw skills and actually develop into really good players. And some of those things that those guys do are really fun to watch."

Witty, urbane and completely at ease in New York's cauldron, Jeter owns this town as a professional and a personality. He is a matinee idol, as the squeals of young girls suggest each time he is introduced at Yankee Stadium.

But make no mistake: there is a serious artist at work here, as much as at any other spot in the Yankee lineup.

Jeter has been the primary piston atop the Yankee lineup while Chuck Knoblauch continues to feel his way. The shortstop seldom misfires, as was shown in a 15-game hitting streak that came to an end last night. He is currently batting .335.

"His potential is unlimited," Ripken said.

The only thing more incredible than Jeter is the fact that he is that hot and still trails Rodriguez in some categories.

Rodriguez, a .313 batter after 198 at-bats, ranked higher than Jeter in runs scored (38), hits (62) and runs batted in (39). He also had 18 doubles and a league-leading .680 slugging percentage.

But more incredibly, in the powerful kingdom of Ken Griffey Jr., Rodriguez led the American League with home runs with 18.

"I think his bat's corked this year," Jeter said with a laugh.

Garciaparra? Last year's A.L. Rookie of the Year had already compiled 44 hits, including five doubles, four triples and five homers, in 147 at-bats before going on the disabled list May 13 with a separated shoulder.

"In the past it was a defensive position," Jeter said. "That's all you had to do. Now if you want to be considered one of the top shortstops, or compete with the other shortstops out there, you have to hit."

Yet the Yankees' leading hitter doesn't completely forget the reason the position exists.

"I still think defense comes first," Jeter said. "When you're playing the middle infield, you're very important to your team and the success of your team is defense. That's the only way you can win is to play good defense."

The marriage of Ozzie Smith's Gold Glove style to Cal Ripken's Silver Slugger is what makes the three gems a special blend.

"I pick up on a lot of subtle things defensively that those guys can do, that they have the skills to do and are learning themselves," Ripken said. "Offense gets them the most attention, but you can see them becoming better and better defensively."

Rodriguez, Jeter and Garciaparra will also benefit from playing against each other.

"It's good to have other shortstops doing well, because then you can't be content," Jeter said. "Having guys around, you're always battling, trying to improve."

Claire Smith

Two of the crown princes at shortstop, Jeter and Alex Rodriguez of the Texas Rangers, have an awkward meeting at second base as Bernie Williams hits into a double play at Yankee Stadium, *Aug. 6, 2003.*
Photo: Barton Silverman, The New York Times

Waiting to Bat

May 31, 1999 | As he waits his turn to bat from the on-deck circle, Derek Jeter glances curiously at the fans sitting in box seats nearby, like a playful seal checking for youngsters outside his pen at the zoo. If somebody engages him, Jeter will answer with a grin. Sometimes he sees a child and asks, "Think I should swing at the first pitch?"

Jeter dives to stop a grounder up the middle by Torii Hunter of the Minnesota Twins in Game 2 of the American League Division Series, *Oct. 2, 2003.*
Photo: Barton Silverman, The New York Times

"He's the best clutch player in baseball. It's tough to describe it to people that don't see him all the time because the stats aren't there. But if you see the day-in, day-out performances, he's the best."

TINO MARTINEZ on Derek Jeter, *April 6, 2005*

Thanks to Jeter (who gets the error), Alex Rodriguez muffs this routine infield fly by the Orioles' Jay Gibbons, allowing a run to score, *Aug. 17, 2006.*
Photo: G. Paul Burnett, The New York Times

"I think you're always looking to improve. Any time you're content with the way that you're playing, that's when you're going to get in trouble. There are so many players you can look at that make you want to improve."

DEREK JETER, *April 14, 1999*

Although Jeter takes out Nick Punto of the Minnesota Twins, he doesn't get the double play, *Oct. 9, 2009.*
Photo: Barton Silverman, The New York Times

The Never-Ending Education of Jeter

March 12, 2000 | The baseball season began for Derek Jeter inside Zuidema Gymnasium, fielding ground balls that skidded across the hardwood floor, taking batting practice against the pitching machine at Kalamazoo Central High School.

Winter's cold lingers in Michigan and Jeter played 20 to 30 games in the spring, more in summer leagues, but not nearly as many as youngsters from the South or the West Coast or the countries of Latin America — where most of his professional peers began playing baseball. In spite of the experience lost to the Midwest climate, he has established himself as one of the game's finest players, and others feel that with additional experience he will inevitably improve even more.

"Before his career is over, he's going to be recognized as one of the best who ever played the game — I really believe that," said Tim Raines, who has played 21 seasons in the big leagues. "You're talking about a guy who batted .349. It's hard to believe he can get better, but I really believe he can."

Raines and others who have watched Jeter, the Yankees shortstop, play daily in recent years believe there are very specific adjustments he can make to his hitting, his fielding, his base running.

Jeter is an aggressive hitter, sometimes with an elementary approach: he makes up his mind about swinging before a pitch is thrown. "Regardless of where it is," Raines said.

The aggressiveness has served him well. If the pitcher is intent on getting ahead in the count and his offering is something Jeter can handle, then Jeter can do great damage. But if the pitch is badly out of the strike zone, or if it is a breaking ball that is moving away from the strike zone, and Jeter does not recognize either, he can be fooled badly.

"When you're going good, when you're in a groove, it's easy to lay off of it," Jeter said. "It's not often during the season that you're that zoned in. You tend to get yourself out. You say to yourself, 'O.K., I'm going to jump on the first pitch,' and you end up swinging at a bad pitch."

Jeter, 25, is such a good hitter that even when fooled, he is capable of hitting a pitch just above his shoes or off the outside corner and dumping a single into right field. But he is also apt to swing at a bad pitch and ground out to second base.

Raines believes that what Jeter will eventually do is to look for one particular type of pitch

Jeter is always working to improve his fielding and hitting — but not everyone is a fan of his spectacular jump-throw plays (opposite).

Photos: Barton Silverman, The New York Times

was on the verge of breaking into the major leagues, and the doubts others expressed about how long it would take for Jeter to develop consistency.

But Jeter has committed only 23 errors over the last two seasons and he has made dramatic progress on fielding balls to his backhand side and charging balls hit in front of him.

"That's one thing that I haven't seen in baseball in all my years," said Sojo, mentioning Jeter's ability to field a ball hit in front of him and throw to first on the run. "This guy is so tall, but he charges the ball with two hands and throws the guy out. Two hands — you don't know how hard that is, and he does it so easy."

Randolph thinks that Jeter could anticipate better on defense, understand better where a hitter is most likely to hit the ball. "And that comes with time, and in knowing the hitters," Randolph said.

Jeter has made a spectacular play in the shortstop hole several times, fielding the ball to his backhand side, then leaping and throwing and cutting down the runner at first. Randolph calls it the Y. A. Tittle play, in honor of the former Giants quarterback, and most of the time, Randolph and Sojo believe Jeter will be better off just planting his right foot, setting his body and throwing, rather than going airborne.

"He's got a great arm," Sojo said. "I'd say to him: 'C'mon, you've got to use your arm. Throw the ball.' When he jumps on that play in the hole and the guy going to first is a good runner, you're not going to get him."

When Jeter joined the Yankees, his fundamentals were ingrained so deeply in his defense that he often tried to reach everything with two hands, including balls hit to his right, and he would reach awkwardly. Randolph does not want him to stop moving his feet and try to reach everything with one

in one particular part of the strike zone early in the count, and look to drive it. And if he does not get that one pitch, then he should let it pass, whether it's a ball or a strike.

The patient approach Raines advocates may be dangerous for a hitter who does not do well when he is behind in the count, someone who is overmatched when he has two strikes against him. But Jeter ranks among the better hitters in baseball when he is behind in the count. According to numbers compiled by Stats Inc., he hit .314 last year in that situation, compared with the American League composite average of .216.

"You go into a series against the Yankees with a plan to pitch to Jeter," Detroit catcher Brad Ausmus said, "and you might get him out in that first game pitching to that hole you think you've seen. But by the last game of the series, that hole isn't there anymore because he will make the adjustments."

Jeter frets about his high number of strikeouts, his former teammate Luis Sojo said — "He'll say, 'Dang, I've got to be leading the league.'" But Raines, the hitting coach Chris Chambliss and Manager Joe Torre do not want him to sacrifice his aggressiveness at the plate merely to decrease his strikeout total. He is undoubtedly improving as a hitter, his average increasing from .314 in his rookie year to .349 last year, his slugging percentage rising 122 points in that time. Chambliss sees him checking his swing more often, recognizing bad pitches more readily.

Willie Randolph, the Yankees' infield coach, believes Jeter is a good shortstop. He remembers the staff meetings when Jeter

hand, but he does think Jeter can trust his hands more than he does, and be a little more fluid, like a Roberto Alomar.

Jeter had just 19 stolen bases last season, sometimes refraining from running in order to keep the first-base hole open — the first baseman had to hold Jeter — for the left-handed-hitting Paul O'Neill. Torre would like to see Jeter run more.

"He could steal 40, 50 bases, I think," Torre said. "But he plays so much, and that wears you out. In that regard, I'm not going to push him to do that, but I certainly want him to not be afraid to make a mistake on the bases. That's one area he's not really as comfortable and confident as I think he should be."

Jeter said: "Base stealing is often the same as defense — you've got to get into a groove, and once you get into a groove, it's a lot easier. One year in the minors, I got into a groove early on and I kept going and going and going."

If Jeter amassed another 15 seasons at his current rate of success, he would approach 4,000 hits and 2,000 runs scored. But there is room for improvement.

Buster Olney

Jeter steals third base (then scores on a balk) in the first inning of a game at Yankee Stadium that the Yankees won, 6-3, against the Baltimore Orioles, *June 3, 2010.*
Photo: Barton Silverman, The New York Times

Hitting Is Uncomplicated Work for Jeter

May 27, 2001 | Derek Jeter has access to volumes of bound scouting reports and stacks of videotapes to study whatever he needs to know about any pitcher the Yankees will face. He can draw from the knowledge of experienced coaches, and also successful and thoughtful teammates.

But hitting is uncomplicated work for Jeter, each at-bat and each hit passing with little recollection or anticipation.

He does not want to know about the pitchers' tendencies, he will not try to guess what they will throw him. It is see the ball, hit the ball, just as it was when he was playing Little League in Michigan.

Jeter cleared his mind in the fourth inning today and sparred with Cleveland's C. C. Sabathia through a 14-pitch plate appearance, the early turning point in the Yankees' 12-5 victory over the Indians at Cleveland.

The Yankees' hitting coach, Gary Denbo, posted the latest intelligence on Sabathia on the lineup card, highlighting in yellow his radar gun times: Fastball, 93-95. Curve, 77-82. Change, 85-86. Before every series, Denbo will give a presentation on the opposing pitchers, based on the reports forwarded to him by the Yankees' advance scouts.

Little of this appeals to Jeter, who watches videotape of his own swing. As he stretches in the on-deck circle, he looks into the scouts' section in the stands, where the Yankees have someone stationed with a radar gun.

Jeter will hold up fingers, guessing how fast the pitcher is throwing — four fingers, for instance, for 94 miles an hour, three fingers for 93 m.p.h. The specific information is relayed back to Jeter, who nods. This is all he wants to know.

Jeter fouled off the first pitch Sabathia threw him, then took a curveball for a ball, fouled off another for a strike, and when the count reached two balls and two strikes, the right-handed-hitting Jeter began slapping foul balls into the stands along the first-base side. His whole approach, he said later, "was to put the ball in play; that's the main thing."

Finally, on the 14th pitch of the at-bat, Jeter took a ball low, drawing the walk on Sabathia's 36th pitch of the inning, his 94th pitch of the game.

Sabathia was ready to be finished, and when he threw a fastball to Paul O'Neill with his next pitch, O'Neill ripped a double into left-center field, two runs scoring.

Buster Olney

Planted in Batter's Box, Jeter Only Sees Red

April 6, 2005 | Derek Jeter does not try to disguise his hitting strategy. He looks for fastballs, whether it is the first inning or the ninth inning, whether he is facing Curt Schilling or Keith Foulke, whether it is the second game in April or the 172nd game in October.

Jeter believes that approach enables him to be ready for a heater and to be poised to react to other pitches. If Jeter sees the red seams of the baseball buzzing toward him like a red dot, he knows it is a slider. If he sees the seams spinning from 12 o'clock to 6 o'clock, he knows it is a curveball.

When Foulke tossed a 3-2 pitch yesterday in the ninth inning of a tie game between the Yankees and the Boston Red Sox, Jeter, as always, was thinking fastball. It did not matter that Foulke had just thrown a changeup, his best pitch, which Jeter fouled off. Jeter does not adjust. He keeps it simple.

Jeter watched the pitch leave Foulke's right hand, quickly detected that the seams were not spinning and were not pressed together and knew it was a fastball. He used his typical inside-out swing, powered the ball to right-center field, saw it sail over the fence and heard an outburst that was part relief and part exhilaration at Yankee Stadium.

After the ball vanished, after he had given the Yankees a 4-3 victory, Jeter pumped his fist. It was a modest celebration.

Jack Curry

Not Surprising

Aug. 20, 2006 | The question put to Derek Jeter, the Yankees' remarkable shortstop: Has anything you have ever done on the field surprised you?

"Yeah," he said, after thinking for a moment. "I think offensively I hit two home runs in the upper deck in right field. That was surprising. One last year and one a few years back. That's probably the most surprising."

What about defensively?

"I don't know if I'd say anything was surprising," he said.

How about his eye-opening play against Oakland in the playoffs in 2001 [see p. 104], when he retrieved an errant throw from right field as he crossed the first-base line? Without turning around, he flipped the ball to the plate, where Jorge Posada tagged Jeremy Giambi and preserved a 1-0 Yankees lead.

"I wasn't surprised by it," Jeter said. "I was supposed to be over there anyway. People think I was completely out of place. That's not the case. The last part of that play I wasn't supposed to do, but I was in the area I was supposed to be in."

All right, how about his catch of Trot Nixon's foul pop in the 12th inning of a 2004 game against Boston [see p. 77] as he ran full speed toward the stands, then hit the low wall as he tumbled hard into the seats?

"That wasn't a surprise," he said. "The aftermath I didn't anticipate. I didn't know it was going to be like that. But the catching the ball part wasn't that difficult. Afterwards it was. I think it was surprising I didn't get hurt more. The catch wasn't surprising."

Murray Chass

Jeter hates missing grounders (left), so he often takes extra workouts, even in bad weather, as he did (opposite) in Fenway Park on Oct. 15, 2004, the day before Game 3 of the American League Championship Series against the Boston Red Sox.
Photos: Vincent Laforet, The New York Times (left); Barton Silverman, The New York Times (opposite)

Extra Practice for Jeter, But No Hint of Doubt

April 18, 2007 | Derek Jeter fielded a grounder and then another and then another. His movements were the same. His glove touched the dirt, his right hand was a few inches above his glove, his knees were bent and his eyes were focused on the approaching ball.

This scene unfolded again and again yesterday at an empty Yankee Stadium. More than three hours before the Yankees played the Cleveland Indians and about an hour before the rest of the Yankees joined Jeter for batting practice, he put in extra work in front of the ushers and security guards.

Jeter insisted it was unrelated to the problems he has endured at shortstop. Jeter has committed six errors in the first 12 games, more than any major leaguer, but he stressed that he often participates in early workouts after a day off.

Still, even if Jeter depicted his actions as normal, there was something noteworthy about a three-time Gold Glove award winner, who is in his 12th season as a starting shortstop, spearing grounders on a barren field and in wet, windy conditions.

Three of Jeter's errors have been on throws and three have been on balls that he bobbled or flubbed. But Jeter emphasized that he did not feel trapped in a slump.

"Do I believe you can be in a defensive slump?" Jeter said. "Yeah, you can. But do I think I'm in one? No."

Jeter has doubters. In the 2007 "Bill James Handbook," there is a statistic called range factor. It is defined as the number of successful chances (putouts plus assists) times nine and divided by the number of innings played. Jeter's range factor was 4.14 in 2006, which was 25th among the 30 regular shortstops in the major leagues.

"They think they have a mathematical equation that figures everything out," Jeter said. "Like every single person is out there with the same runner and the same pitcher and the ball is hit in the same exact place. It seems like once somebody says one thing about you, people tend to run with it and we never hear the end of it."

Manager Joe Torre said he was not concerned with Jeter's defense and instead lauded the intangibles he offers.

"The lack of fear and the lack of being afraid to fail is, to me, it works to his advantage," Torre said.

Jeter stood yesterday in the infield where the grass first touches the dirt. He fielded 12 grounders flawlessly. Then Jeter retreated to his normal depth and fielded 31 more grounders without a miscue.

Jack Curry

Sunshine Amid Clouds

May 13, 2007 | Three hours before Friday night's game, Jeter stood in the middle of the visiting locker room at Safeco Field in Seattle with a soft-serve ice cream cone. It made him look carefree, which in many ways he is.

"You can tell he enjoys every aspect of the game," said first baseman Doug Mientkiewicz, who is playing on a team with Jeter for the first time this season. "The good, the bad and the ugly, he thoroughly enjoys all of it."

For the Yankees, there have been plenty of bad and ugly. But aside from a brief fielding slump in early April, not much of it has been caused by Jeter. He leads the American League in batting average (.376) and hits (53), maintaining a sunny outlook.

"I'm optimistic by nature," he said. "Even when things are going poorly, you've got to find something positive. You have to. Because if you get caught up in being negative all the time, you'll never get out of any kind of funk."

Jeter is not immune to slumps, of course. He went 0 for 32 early in the 2004 season. But he has been remarkably consistent over the past two seasons. At one point, from Aug. 20, 2006,

through May 3, 2007, he had at least one hit in 59 of 61 games. The stretch began with a 25-game hitting streak, followed by a hitless game. A 14-game hitting streak followed that. Then, after another hitless game, Jeter ripped off 20 in a row.

According to Trent McCotter of the Society for American Baseball Research, only one other player since 1900 had as many as 59 games out of 61 with a hit: Joe DiMaggio, who hit safely in 60 of 61 in 1941, when he had a record 56-game streak.

"I don't think about it, really," Jeter said. "All I try to do, pretty much, is to be consistent. I don't try to overanalyze anything, I don't try to sit back and say, You're doing this or that. I just try to consistently help out every day."

History shows that he does not vary much from the way he starts a season. Only once has Jeter's season-ending batting average been more than .013 below his average May 11. And that year (1999), he finished second in the league in hitting at .349.

Tyler Kepner

Jeter Lets Chance to Know What's Coming Sail On By

June 16, 2007 | Derek Jeter had a chance for some authentic, inside information about how another major league team planned to pitch him. But Jeter, the Yankees' shortstop, refused to listen yesterday.

"I don't want to know," Jeter said. "As far as what pitchers do, I really don't care. All I want to know is what they've got. I don't get into all that stuff. It makes you think too much. I don't want to think."

When the Arizona Diamondbacks left Yankee Stadium on Thursday, they left behind their scouting report of the Yankees' hitters. The Associated Press found the report on the floor of the visitors' dugout and published it.

The Diamondbacks' report said that Jeter struggled with pitches down and in and chased sliders away. The report urged pitchers to mix

locations and types of pitches on the first pitch because Jeter is an aggressive hitter.

Jeter, though, said he never tried to guess along with a pitcher. He said that he looked for a fastball on every pitch and reacted to breaking balls. If he tried to anticipate other pitches, he said, he would be prone to swinging at balls.

"If you're pitching against me, tell me what's coming," Jeter said. "I wouldn't want to know. If I look for, like, a curveball? As soon as I see it, no matter where it is, I'll swing at it."

Tyler Kepner

Swing Science: The Fine Points

June 1, 2008 | "Hitting the other way" is a skill that prevents defenders from shading a batter to one side of the field, and makes it harder for pitchers to get batters out by working the outside of the plate. To hit the other way, most batters counter their instinct to pull the ball by swinging later at a pitch, preferably at one on the far corner. The bat meets the ball at an angle that sends it toward that side of the field.

Some batters close their stance slightly, meaning they move their front foot a few inches closer to the plate than their back foot; this keeps their hips and shoulders from "flying open" and positions them to drive the ball the other way.

While most batters are able to go the other way on an outside pitch, the Yankees' Derek Jeter has made a career out of doing it with inside pitches as well. He pulls his hands close to his body and keeps them stiff as he swings, so the head of the bat lags behind the handle, at an angle facing right field.

Pat Borzi

This inside-out swing allows Jeter to go the other way with inside pitches, too.
Photo: Richard Perry, The New York Times

A Rarity

May 29, 2008 | An oddity in the Yankees' game against the Orioles Tuesday in Baltimore was the pickoff of Derek Jeter by the Orioles' Dennis Sarfate.

According to the Elias Sports Bureau, it was the first time Jeter had been picked off since Sept. 2, 1998, by Oakland's Gil Heredia.

Jeter catches a throw
from first baseman Andy
Phillips and stretches
to second base for the
force-out on the Atlanta
Braves' Ryan Langerhans,
June 27, 2006.
Photo: Barton Silverman,
The New York Times

An Instinctual Play

Aug. 10, 2009 | As Derek Jeter saw Kevin Youkilis flying toward him with a takeout slide Saturday, he made a clever decision. Jeter jumped completely over Youkilis's beefy body, landed and then fired to first to complete the double play. Because the runner chugging to first was the slow-footed Mike Lowell, Jeter knew he had the extra time.

It was an instinctual play, the kind that Jeter has made over and over during his career with the Yankees. There are lots of players with better statistics than Jeter, but there are only a few who are as smart. Those heady plays help show why Jeter is so valuable to the Yankees.

Jeter Keeps Hitting, With No Plans on Moving

Aug. 20, 2009 | Derek Jeter was the Yankees' designated hitter on Monday in Oakland, Calif., and he joked with Manager Joe Girardi that it was such an easy workday, he could do it for five years.

"It's easier to D.H.," Jeter said. "You only have to worry about one thing."

That was a typical comment from Jeter, simple and irrefutable. He is still very much a shortstop, happy to be there with no intention of moving. And the way he is hitting, he must feel as if he could hit forever.

Through Tuesday, Jeter was riding his hottest stretch at the plate in six years. He was 20 for 36 (.556) over his last nine games, including five games with at least three hits.

"It just seems like every swing he takes, he's getting a good pitch to hit and he's not missing it," the hitting coach Kevin Long said. "His strike-zone discipline has been something that's been really, really good. I used to see him expand the zone quite a bit more, and I just don't see that."

Jeter was pleasant but brief Wednesday in talking about himself. He is rarely introspective, and keeping things uncomplicated helps make him successful. But there are reasons he is better this season, reasons he is swinging at better pitches.

"The better you feel, the more comfortable you feel, the better you are swinging at pitches," he said. "When you don't feel as good at the plate, a lot of times you chase pitches. So I think it's just a matter of how you feel results in the pitches you swing at, and the better pitches you swing at, the better your results will be."

Jeter rarely offers specifics about his physical condition, good or bad, but he worked on the lower half of his body last winter and has looked more nimble. He gets to more balls in the field, by all accounts, and has taken to the leadoff spot with 20 stolen bases.

"You always switch up your workout routine," Jeter said. "But you go through the course of a season, some things happen. You may hurt something, you may not feel as good. I've been fortunate so far this year, I guess."

Long said Jeter had made only one mechanical change, concentrating on squaring his feet to the pitcher. Last season, he was a bit open or closed at times. The adjustment, Long said, makes him more direct to the ball.

As for the leadoff spot, Long guessed that Jeter might be more aware of the need to get on base than he was before. His on-base percentage from the leadoff spot, .398, ranks second among major league leadoff batters. But Jeter said his spot in the order was meaningless.

"Nothing different hitting first or second except the fact that you hit about two minutes earlier," Jeter said. "Really, no difference — zero. I change absolutely nothing no matter where I am in the lineup."

Jeter had more than 400 career games batting leadoff before this season, so the spot was familiar to him, and he has not changed.

That has worked for Jeter for nearly 14 full seasons, each with at least 150 hits, the longest such streak among active players and the longest in Yankees history. He is showing no signs of slowing, and at 35, Jeter said he had given no thought to how long he wanted to keep playing.

All he knows, he said, is that he will play as long as he has fun. It is clear, too, that he will not leave shortstop for a long time. A reporter asked if he could see himself as a full-time designated hitter at age 41, and Jeter replied, "You'll see me at short still."

What about designated hitter at 46 years old?

"Maybe," Jeter said.

Tyler Kepner

"Greatest catch I've ever seen. It was unbelievable. He's just so unselfish. He put his body in a compromising spot. It was hard to watch."

ALEX RODRIGUEZ after Derek Jeter's running catch propelled him into the seats, *July 2, 2004*

CHAPTER ❸

SEASONS

When Derek Jeter broke a hitless streak of 32 at-bats in April 2004, it was front-page news in The Times. Such was the anomaly of a player who had nearly captured the American League batting title the previous season but was struggling so badly the next.

Of course, Jeter recovered to finish around his usual statistical levels, carrying the Yankees into October again. It is what the great ones do — establish a high standard of performance and play to it year after year, as long as they stay healthy.

Jeter has been fortunate to avoid major injuries, but some of his luck is by design. He plays through most inconveniences, and loathes talking about physical problems. As he has reminded reporters, there is a difference between being injured and being hurt. Everybody, Jeter says, gets hurt.

Jeter separated his shoulder on opening night in 2003, in a collision at third base in Toronto, but otherwise he has missed only small chunks of time here and there. In 2000, when most of baseball's big names skipped the All-Star Game in Atlanta — were they injured, or simply hurt? — Jeter provided the star power with three hits and received the game's Most Valuable Player award.

The M.V.P. award for the regular season has eluded Jeter, but his durability and dependability annually produce impressive numbers — often 200 hits, usually a .300 average and 100 runs scored, with respectable extra-base pop. Yet for Jeter, who measures success solely by championships, it is all just a tune-up for autumn.

Fans and teammates
help Derek Jeter after
his full-speed catch of
a fly ball by Trot Nixon
of the Boston Red Sox
propelled him into the
stands, *July 1, 2004.*
Photo: Jason Szenes,
European Pressphoto Agency

The Streak Without a Record

May 28, 1999 | At Yankee Stadium last night, the primary plot was not merely Roger Clemens's first start as a Yankee against the Red Sox but also his success in extending his streak of consecutive victories to 19 over two seasons. But a strange streak also was extended. With two singles last night, Derek Jeter has now been on base in each of the Yankees' 45 games this season.

Clemens knows the major league record he was approaching: Carl Hubbell's 24 consecutive victories for the New York Giants from July 17, 1936, to May 27, 1937.

But for Jeter's streak, no record exists. Of the thousands of records in "The Book of Baseball Records," the blue-covered bible published annually by the Elias Sports Bureau, there is no record for "consecutive games, on base safely." And there may never be one.

"You'd have to have a play-by-play of every major league game going all the way back more than 100 years," said Seymour Siwoff, the Elias emperor and the keeper of the keys to baseball records. "And nobody has that."

During an inquiring conversation with Siwoff yesterday, it was established that Joe DiMaggio was on base safely in 74 consecutive games in 1941, a streak created primarily by his most memorable record: hitting safely in 56 consecutive games that season.

"But DiMaggio's 74 games may not be the major league record," Siwoff said. "It might not even be the Yankee record. Because nobody knows what the record is."

By clicking their computers, the Elias figure filberts were able to certify that Jeter's streak was the longest for a Yankee going back to the 1961 season.

But somewhere sometime another Yankee or another major leaguer might have put together more than the 74 games in DiMaggio's on-base streak.

Dave Anderson

> "It bothers me more that we lost. You don't think about that, you just try to get on base."
>
> **DEREK JETER** after the Mets halted his on-base streak at 53 straight games, *June 7, 1999*

200 Hits Again

Sept. 19, 1999 | The Indians won the game, 5-4, in Cleveland. Derek Jeter went 3 for 4 and has 201 hits, after accumulating 203 last season. He is the first Yankee since Don Mattingly (1984-86) to reach that mark in consecutive seasons.

Career Highs

Oct. 4, 1999 | Derek Jeter hit .349 and finished second to Boston's Nomar Garciaparra in the A.L. batting race. Jeter also established career highs in doubles (37), triples (9), home runs (24), runs batted in (102), hits (219) and walks (91). He has 807 career hits. He is 25 years old.

> "He'll be doing a lot of things that will make you go back to the record book."
>
> **MANAGER JOE TORRE** on Derek Jeter's second straight 200-hit season, *Sept. 19, 1999*

Jeter and Jorge Posada get ready for a workout at Turner Field in Atlanta before the All-Star Game, July 10, 2000.

Photo: Harry How, Allsport

Jeter Gives the Fans an All-Star Performance

July 12, 2000 | Derek Jeter tucked his jersey into his uniform pants and listed the people who were at the All-Star Game to watch him start for the American League tonight. Jeter mentioned his parents, his sister and three of his friends from New York, shaking his head as he talked about securing enough decent tickets. But Jeter should not have stopped his list at six people.

There were 51,317 other fans who were at Turner Field in Atlanta to watch him, too. It happened that way because a game that was missing marquee players like Mark McGwire, Ken Griffey Jr., Alex Rodriguez and Pedro Martinez, and was being called the All-Scar Game, developed into another enticing stage for the amazing Jeter.

Jeter stroked three hits, knocked in two runs and scored one run to power the American League past the National League, 6-3, and become the first Yankee to win the Most Valuable Player award in the All-Star Game. Manager Joe Torre chose his shortstop as the starter after Rodriguez sustained a concussion last Friday, and Jeter poked a two-run single off the Mets'

Al Leiter in the fourth inning to break a 1-1 tie in helping the A.L. win the game for the fourth straight year.

"You have to play a lot of years before you can be considered a Yankee great," Jeter said. "This is my fifth year. Hopefully, I can play a few more years and start that debate."

The debate has already started. Yogi Berra, Mickey Mantle, Roger Maris, Reggie Jackson, Thurman Munson, Dave Winfield, Reggie Jackson, Don Mattingly, Rickey Henderson, Paul O'Neill and Mariano Rivera have all played in All-Star Games as Yankees since the M.V.P. was first given in 1962, but none ever won what Jeter did tonight. The National Baseball Hall of Fame took Jeter's black Louisville Slugger P72 bat that he used for all three hits back to Cooperstown, N.Y.

"Right now, I'm very happy, obviously," Jeter said. "And I wasn't aware that no other Yankee had won this award, and it's kind of hard to believe."

Jack Curry

"I feel just like a little kid. I always used to watch the game with my father."

DEREK JETER after being added to his first All-Star team, as a reserve shortstop (he played three innings, handled two groundouts, and struck out in his one at-bat), *July 2, 1998*

200 Hits, Three Years in a Row

Oct. 1, 2000 | Derek Jeter singled in the fourth inning to reach 200 hits for the third consecutive year. Jeter is the third player in club history to do so, joining Lou Gehrig (1927-29) and Don Mattingly (1984-86). In the last 50 years, only three American League players other than Jeter and Mattingly have totaled 200 or more hits in three straight years: Jim Rice, Wade Boggs and Kirby Puckett.

Triumph and Cheers Greet Yanks in Return

Sept. 19, 2001 | Flag-waving fans in Chicago wiped away tears and loudly sang "God Bless America," and when first baseman Paul Konerko failed to scoop a throw out of the dirt and allowed the Yankees to score a first-inning run, the fans came together in heart and soul again. They groaned, in perfect harmony.

The Yankees, playing their first game since the Sept. 11 horror, romped over Chicago, 11-3; Alfonso Soriano, Jorge Posada and Shane Spencer hit homers. But White Sox fans didn't seem to take it personally. "We love you, New York!" a man bellowed through silence as the colors were marched onto the field before the game, and other fans among the crowd of 22,785 roared approvingly.

The Yankees stood on the foul lines before the game and wore the hats of the New York Fire and Police Departments, as the Mets had in Pittsburgh on Monday night. There was a moment of silence, the national anthem was sung and fans chanted "U.S.A.!" Several Yankees wept; Manager Joe Torre returned to his office to compose himself before the game started.

"People responded so great," Bernie Williams said. "I never heard White Sox fans rooting for us."

The Yankees had won 9 of their last 10 games before everything stopped last week, and once they resumed tonight, it was as if nothing had changed. Chuck Knoblauch singled on the seventh pitch of the game, Derek Jeter singled, Tino Martinez pulled a single to right field, and Jeter crossed the plate with the game's first run, slapping Posada's outstretched hand.

The Yankees piled on runs in the last innings, Posada crushing a grand slam in the seventh, Jeter finishing the game with three hits.

But judging by the reception the Yankees received here tonight, others will see the interlocking N and Y on the caps of the Yankees, the words "New York" extended across their road jerseys, and it's inevitable that the Yankees will be viewed as representatives of a devastated and resilient city.

Buster Olney

100 Runs, 7 Times

Aug. 27, 2002 | Derek Jeter scored his 100th and 101st runs of the season. He joined Ted Williams (1939-49) of the Red Sox and Earle Combs (1925-32) of the Yankees as the only players in modern history to score at least 100 runs in their first seven seasons.

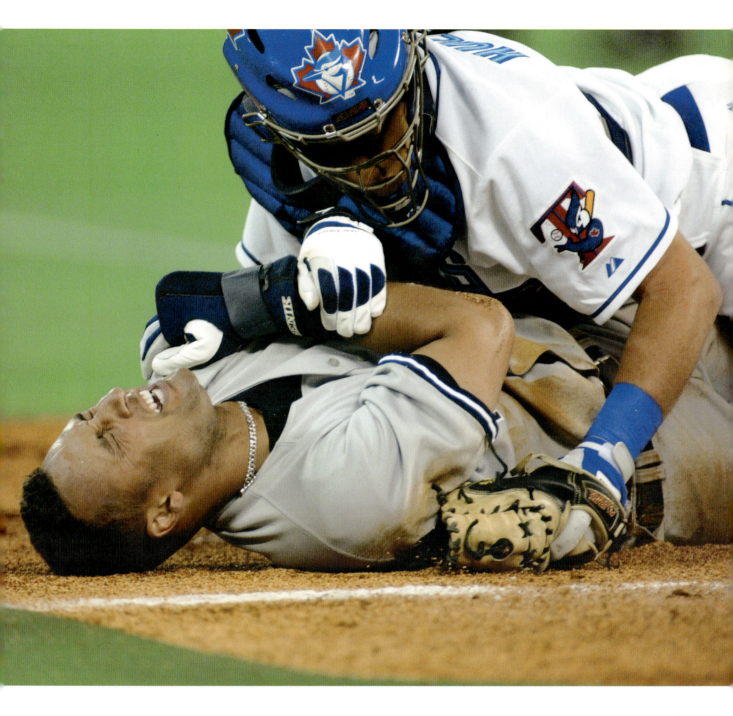

Agony on Opening Day

April 1, 2003 | They huddled by third base for 12 minutes, watching their team leader writhing and wailing. Derek Jeter was in teeth-grinding pain, and the Yankees' season changed just as it began.

It should have been a blissful opening night in Toronto for the Yankees, who hung on to beat the Toronto Blue Jays, 8-4. Roger Clemens worked six shutout innings for his 294th career victory, Robin Ventura hit a two-run homer and Alfonso Soriano belted his first career grand slam.

But the Yankees' joy was stifled by concern for Jeter, who will go on the disabled list after dislocating his left shoulder in a collision at third base with Toronto catcher Ken Huckaby. Yankees Manager Joe Torre said he expected Jeter to miss at least a month.

Jeter reacts after dislocating his left shoulder in a collision with Toronto Blue Jays catcher Ken Huckaby at third base, *March 31, 2003.*
Photo: Rick Stewart, Getty Images

Wearing a Trenton
Thunder uniform, Jeter
warms up during
a five-game rehab stint
with the AA team in New
Jersey, *May 7, 2003.*
Photo: Tim Shaffer for The
New York Times

"It's going to take a while, I guess," Jeter said after returning from a hospital. "When it first happened, I didn't know what to expect. I felt it pop out, but the painful part is getting it back in."

Yankee trainers and Blue Jay doctors tried to pop it back. They could not, and after a delay in getting a cart to the field, Jeter was taken to the Yankees' clubhouse, where his shoulder was put back in place.

Jeter had X-rays, which showed no break, but he will have a magnetic resonance imaging test on Tuesday. If the results show a severe dislocation, Jeter could miss the season.

Jeter's left arm was in a sling after the game, and though he said he would return this year, he admitted his shoulder "hurts just sitting there." On Sunday, Torre said Jeter was as strong physically as he had been in years. That changed tonight.

"This kid never shows any pain," Torre said. "He's played with pain I can't tell you how many times, and not let on. But this was something he couldn't hide."

Jeter sustained the injury on an unusual play in the third inning after drawing a one-out walk. With Jason Giambi, a pull hitter, batting, the Blue Jays shifted their infielders to the right side, leaving third base uncovered.

Giambi bounced softly to the pitcher, Roy Halladay, who threw to first baseman Carlos Delgado for an out. Jeter crossed second and kept running, expecting no fielder to cover third.

The strategy worked for Jeter in a game here last August, but the Blue Jays were prepared this time. Huckaby raced down the third base line as Delgado fired across the infield. Huckaby caught the ball just as Jeter slid headfirst, and the umpire Paul Emmel signaled safe.

But Huckaby could not stop his momentum. After catching the high throw, he careered into Jeter with his knees, his shinguards crashing into Jeter's left shoulder. Jeter's helmet flew off and he instantly grabbed his shoulder. He was knocked off the base and Huckaby tagged him, ending the inning.

Asked if Huckaby's play was dirty, Jeter said: "I don't know, it's tough. He was running full speed trying to get to third base."

Huckaby called Jeter during the game and left a message in the Yankees' clubhouse. He said he intended no harm.

Tyler Kepner

Going the opposite way,
Jeter singles in a run
against the Anaheim
Angels, his first hit in his
first game after being out
for about six weeks with
a dislocated shoulder,
May 13, 2003.
Photo: Barton Silverman,
The New York Times

Jeter and Yanks Get on Track

May 16, 2003 | Derek Jeter gave himself a one-clap round of applause when he arrived at second base in the third inning last night. He had driven in his first run of the season with his second double of the game.

Jeter also singled in the fifth inning and the Yankees finally won with him in the lineup, a 10-4 rout of the Anaheim Angels last night at Yankee Stadium. Jeter has 7 hits in 14 at-bats since he rejoined the Yankees on Tuesday. He missed six weeks with a dislocated left shoulder, but he seems just fine now.

"I'm good enough," he said.

Jeter seemed to relish the postgame handshake with his teammates. He remembered that he had not participated in such a tradition since October.

"Hopefully, things are back to normal," Jeter said.

Dave Caldwell

No Batting Title, But Still Satisfied

Sept. 29, 2003 | Derek Jeter missed out on a personal accomplishment. Jeter entered the game with a .326 average, a point behind Boston's Bill Mueller in the American League batting race. Jeter went 0 for 3 and lost out to Mueller, who pinch hit for the Red Sox at Tampa Bay and went 0 for 1. Jeter finished with a .324 average, a 27-point improvement from last season.

"I'm more pleased with this season than any other season, because it's been tougher, injury-wise," Jeter said. "It's probably more satisfying than any year before."

"A streak like that, you wouldn't wish on anyone," Jeter said. "Even guys on the other team have been supportive. It's rough when you're going through it, but you're the only one that can get yourself out of it."

Since his rookie season in 1996, Jeter has 1,549 hits, the most in that span in the major leagues, according to the Elias Sports Bureau. But for eight games, the man with an average annual salary of almost $19 million could not buy a hit.

Jeter's slump defied explanation. It was the longest by a Yankee since Jimmy Wynn went 0 for 32 in 1977, and for part of it, the fans had booed Jeter in frustration, especially during last weekend's sweep by the Red Sox. By Tuesday, the fans were cheering him again, standing during his at-bats and chanting his name.

"They probably started feeling sorry for me a little bit," Jeter said. "But even when they booed me before, they were still cheering when I went to the plate."

Jeter acknowledged the fans last night with a quick wave from the top step of the dugout after his home run. He went 1 for 4 over all.

Tyler Kepner

Jeter, Anemic at 0 for 32, Is a Crusher at 1 for 33

April 30, 2004 | Yogi Berra has forgotten some details, but he knew the length of his worst hitless streak, the way he broke out of it and the opponent when he did. Decades later, Derek Jeter provided the historical symmetry to an epic slump.

In his first at-bat against the Oakland Athletics' Barry Zito last night, Jeter crushed a first-pitch homer deep over the left-center-field wall near Monument Park at Yankee Stadium. The blast emphatically ended a slide that had reached 0 for 32, a figure that was familiar to Berra, the Yankee Hall of Famer.

"It's funny," Berra said before last night's game, a 7-5 Yankee victory. "I went 0 for 32 once. I hit a home run the next time up." The home run, he added, was against the Kansas City Athletics, a forerunner of the Oakland team.

The way things were going, Jeter said, he wondered if his ball would collide with a bird and land in an outfielder's glove. Since his leadoff infield single in Chicago on April 20, nothing had gone right for Jeter.

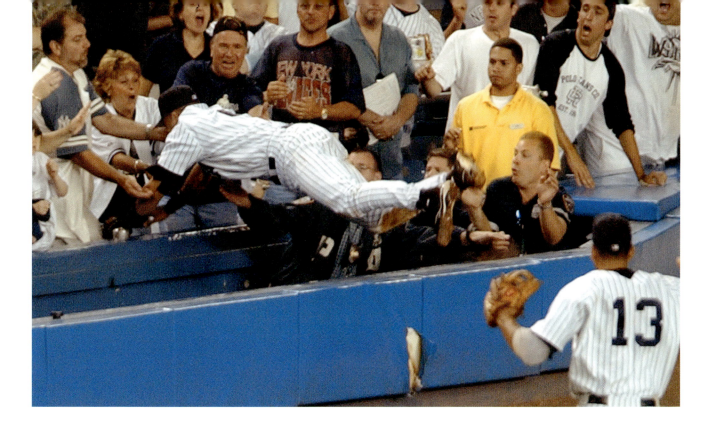

Dust Settles in 13th, and Yankees Sweep

July 2, 2004 | Only the calendar kept last night's game at Yankee Stadium from standing among the most electrifying in baseball history. There were battered heroes and brushback pitches, missed opportunities and clutch hits. There was Alex Rodriguez playing shortstop and Gary Sheffield playing third base.

And in the end, with Derek Jeter at a hospital after crash-landing in the seats for a game-saving catch an inning earlier, there was John Flaherty, the last man on the bench, rifling the game-winning hit down the left-field line in the bottom of the 13th inning for a 5-4 victory.

"That was the greatest game I've ever watched, played or been in the ballpark for," Rodriguez said. "It was an unbelievable war."

It was a haunting scene for the Red Sox and a pulsating one for the Yankees, who sealed a rollicking three-game sweep and opened a season-high eight-and-a-half-game lead in the American League East. A Yankees-Red Sox game in extra innings in the Bronx was almost bound to turn out like this.

In the top of the 12th, Jeter was the Yankees' only hope. Trot Nixon's soft fly ball was falling fast, and no other fielder was close to it. Jeter raced to his right and added to his legend.

With two outs and a runner at third, a hit would have given the Red Sox the lead. But there was Jeter, sprinting and swiping the ball from the air in fair territory. Unable to stop his momentum, he tumbled into the seats, spikes high, several rows back.

Rodriguez followed Jeter and waved for help. As a trainer went onto the field, Jeter emerged from among the fans — his fans — and stood above them for a moment as he climbed a wall to get back on the field. There was blood on his jersey, blood on his right cheek, blood on his chin. It was Jeter to the rescue.

The Yankees said he sustained a laceration of his chin, a bruised right cheek and a bruised right shoulder. Posada said Jeter had stitches on his chin. Jeter told Posada he would play at Shea Stadium tonight.

"I've never seen a guy of his caliber go all out," Sheffield said. "It proved to you how important these games are. It took our captain to prove it to us again."

Tyler Kepner

▲ Jeter plunges into the stands at Yankee Stadium after racing to catch a fly ball in the 12th inning of a game against the Boston Red Sox, *July 1, 2004.*
Photo: Frank Franklin II, Associated Press

◄ Jeter strikes out (opposite, left) for the third time in a game against the Boston Red Sox, April 25, 2004 — but four days later ends his 0-for-32 slump by hitting a home run (opposite, right).
Photos: Barton Silverman, The New York Times

"I always play hard.
That's your job,
to lead by example.
If it makes other
people want to play
hard and win more,
I guess it's worth it."

DEREK JETER on his catch, *July 3, 2004*

A bruised but unbowed
Jeter displays good cheer
and his badge of honor
a day after his running
catch landed him in the
stands, *July 2, 2004.*
Photo: Keith Bedford for
The New York Times

Jeter's Catch Shows Unique Instinct and Ability

July 3, 2004 | It seems so elementary, and to Derek Jeter, it is: he is on the field to win, and he will adjust to the situation to meet that goal. Other hitters are more menacing, other fielders more sparkling, but few, if any, are as adaptable as Jeter.

Last week in Baltimore, he beat the Orioles with a home run over the center-field fence. He stole two bases in the Yankees' victory over Boston on Tuesday. On Wednesday night, he put down a crucial sacrifice bunt to help the Yankees win. Then came Thursday, when Jeter made a play that will likely be remembered for years in what was one of the most riveting games in memory.

"This was the most exciting game I have ever seen in all of sports," the Yankees' principal owner, George Steinbrenner, said in a statement, and the seminal moment belonged to Jeter, the captain, whom he called "an inspiration for all of our nation's youth."

There was Jeter, when the Yankees needed him most, making a play few shortstops could make. There was Jeter, with the game in the balance in the 12th inning against the Red Sox, sprinting and stretching and crashing into the stands, his face a wreck but Trot Nixon's fair ball nestled in his glove.

Jeter could have been a mother bird swooping for an egg falling from a nest. It was all instinct, the Yankees thought, something inside Jeter that few athletes possess.

"He knew, as he went after that ball, that he had a decision to make," said Tony Clark, who watched the play unfold from first base. "Either you let the ball drop and try to minimize the damage, or you make the catch and pay the consequences. He knew that, no doubt about it, and he chose B."

Alex Rodriguez, who followed Jeter into the stands and waved frantically for a trainer, said he would not have been surprised if Jeter had broken his jaw or separated his shoulder on the play.

"He looked like he got hit by Mike Tyson," Rodriguez said.

When Jeter emerged woozily from the stands, he had blood on his face, chin and jersey. But the consequences were not serious, considering the force of impact. He was at Columbia-Presbyterian Center of New York-Presbyterian Hospital when the Yankees came back to win, despite trailing by a run with two outs and no base runners in the 13th inning.

He was back in the lineup against the Mets last night, as he had promised teammate Jorge Posada he would be the night before.

Reporters swarmed Jeter's locker at Shea Stadium before the game last night, and the first question was, "What hurts?"

Jeter replied with the only answer he gives in these situations: "Nothing."

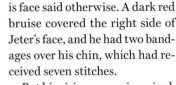

His face said otherwise. A dark red bruise covered the right side of Jeter's face, and he had two bandages over his chin, which had received seven stitches.

But his vision was unimpaired, and that was all the Yankees had worried about. "I'm fine," Jeter insisted.

Jeter dislocated his left shoulder on opening night in Toronto last season, and he told Manager Joe Torre he could play the next game. He could not, of course; the injury cost him six weeks. When he dashed for the ball on Thursday night, having shaded the pull-hitting Nixon up the middle, Jeter had the presence of mind to consider his shoulder.

"I tried to turn and jump to my right so I wouldn't hurt my left shoulder," he said.

Yankees General Manager Brian Cashman said the team would have been devastated to lose the game after Jeter's selflessness. Several teammates said they were inspired by Jeter's display, that it was the definition of his role as captain.

Who else would have attempted the play, knowing how badly he could have been hurt? "A utility player trying to stay in the league," Gary Sheffield said. "Those are probably the only guys."

Tyler Kepner

Jeter Wins His First Gold Glove

Nov. 3, 2004 | It is a pastime among baseball statisticians to malign Derek Jeter's defense. Two years ago, when Jeter said he wanted to win a Gold Glove at shortstop, he was roundly ridiculed.

But yesterday, Rawlings announced that Jeter had won his first Gold Glove award, voted on by American League managers and coaches. Alex Rodriguez had won the last two, but Rodriguez moved to third base when he joined the Yankees.

Jeter reached far more balls this season than he did in 2003, when his opening-day shoulder injury may have limited his range to his left. Jeter's range factor (putouts plus assists times nine, divided by innings) was 4.46, up from 3.75 the year before.

"It's a great honor," Jeter said in a statement. "I take pride in my defense, and I work hard each year to improve in the field. There are a number of fantastic defensive shortstops in the American League — too many to count — and to be recognized with the Gold Glove makes it that much more of an accomplishment.

"I also want to thank our pitching staff for having so many of our opponents hit balls in my direction."

Tyler Kepner

One Swing, Four Runs, and a Streak Vanishes

June 19, 2005 | The bases were loaded for the Yankees with one out in the top of the sixth inning yesterday at the Stadium. Derek Jeter, who has done virtually everything for the Yankees in his nine-plus years with the team — except, well, one thing — came to bat against the Chicago Cubs.

What Jeter — the shortstop with few peers — had never done was hit a home run with the bases loaded in the major leagues.

In fact, he had the most home runs hit by an active player without having whacked one over the fence with three men on. It was the most, for that matter, of any Yankee, ever. One hundred and fifty-six homers, some when the game was on the line, but never with the bases jammed.

"Guys would get on me about it," Jeter said regarding ribbing from his teammates. "And three or four years ago, I don't remember exactly when, Mark McLemore had the longest streak. But he had hit one the day before we got into Seattle. And when he saw me, he said, 'Now you have the record.'" Jeter smiled wanly when he recalled it.

The Cubs replaced the left-handed reliever Rich Hill with a right-hander, Joe Borowski, to face the right-handed-batting Jeter.

"I wasn't thinking home run," Jeter said. "I mean, I had thought that I would never hit one. Right at that moment, I just wanted to hit a fly ball to get the runner in from third. I was trying to avoid hitting a ground ball."

Borowski threw, Jeter swung, and the ball soared toward center field. "I hit it good," Jeter said, "but I thought it was high. I didn't know if it was going out."

The Cubs' center fielder, Corey Patterson, began to run for the ball but quickly saw that his effort was futile. The ball sailed over the fence, and as Jeter rounded the bases, jubilant in his heart but still professionally cool as cauliflower, the capacity crowd of 55,284 rose and cheered.

The scoreboard read Yankees 7, Cubs 1.

The fans, meanwhile, would not let up with their cries of delight, even as Tony Womack, the next batter, took his place in the batter's box. "De-rek Je-ter! De-rek Je-ter!" they chanted. They were demanding a curtain call. And the manager came to their aid. "I had to kind of push him out," Joe Torre said.

Ira Berkow

"Nothing is sweeter than Derek Jeter."

HOMEMADE SIGN CARRIED BY A YOUNG GIRL
at Yankee Stadium, *Aug. 14, 1998*

From the beginning,
Jeter has attracted a
fervent following, par-
ticularly among young
women and teen-age
girls — many of whom
display high hopes of
being the one to end his
bachelor status.
Photos: Chang W. Lee,
The New York Times (left);
Robert Caplin, The New
York Times (below)

Jeter fans, especially females, covet his autograph (and any other tokens of his appreciation).

Photos: Tim Shaffer for The New York Times (above); Barton Silverman, The New York Times (right)

Boston Ends Jeter's Streak

Sept. 18, 2006 | The Yankees could have eliminated Boston from the playoff race by winning three of four games over the last two days. Instead, it was the Red Sox who took three of four, including both games yesterday (6-3 and 5-4). In the process, they put an end to Derek Jeter's 25-game hitting streak, the longest by a Yankee in 64 years.

In his fourth and final at-bat last night, Jeter swung at a 3-0 pitch for the first time since 2002, grounding out to first in the seventh inning to finish 0 for 4. Jeter's hitting streak was the Yankees' longest since Joe Gordon hit safely in 29 consecutive games in 1942.

Jeter Blast Silences Fenway Crowd

Sept. 17, 2007 | In their final meeting of the regular season, the Yankees nipped the Red Sox, 4-3, in Boston, getting two home runs off Curt Schilling and a strong return by Roger Clemens on Sunday night. Robinson Cano hit the first homer and Derek Jeter the second — a two-out, three-run blast over the Green Monster in the eighth inning that will rattle around New England brains until the Yankees' season is over.

"He's got one good knee, and he's still the best clutch hitter I've ever seen," Clemens said of Jeter, who was 6 for 30 on this trip before he connected.

This game was a preview of October drama at its best. It ended with David Ortiz at the plate against Mariano Rivera with two outs and the bases loaded.

With a 2-2 count, Rivera jammed Ortiz with a cutter, and the best he could do was pop it into shallow center. Jeter — who else? — ranged out to corral it, pumping his fist after ending the game.

"Ever since you're a little kid, you think about being up in a big situation," Jeter said. "I think you always envision yourself coming through."

Schilling entered the eighth having thrown only 69 pitches. He had set down the next 10 hitters after Cano's home run, but Doug Mientkiewicz looped a single to left with one out in the eighth.

Jason Giambi drove a pinch-hit single off the top of the Monster, and after a broken-bat groundout by Damon, Schilling tried splitters and fastballs against Jeter, who got ahead in the count, before fouling off two pitches.

Then came the hit that silenced Fenway, a sizzler through the sky off a 2-2 splitter and a dagger through the Red Sox. It was a Jeter special, extraordinary and routine all at once.

Tyler Kepner

> "It's scary, but you expect it. He just finds a way to have his best at-bat when you need it most."

DOUG MIENTKIEWICZ after Derek Jeter's game-winning home run, *Sept. 17, 2007*

"I love it. If anyone's going to hit a game-winning home run for the first win at the new stadium, it's going to be Derek."

MARK TEIXEIRA, after the Yankees beat the Cleveland Indians, 6-5, on Derek Jeter's eighth-inning home run off Jensen Lewis, *April 18, 2009*

The Yankees Take a Page from the Past

July 9, 2008 | Andy Pettitte punched the thick air with his fist, then slapped his left hand against his glove. With one play, he had hopped into a time machine, when Derek Jeter had limitless range and the Tampa Bay Rays tried in vain to catch the Yankees.

At 34, Jeter does not move as quickly as he once did. With the best record in baseball, the Rays are no longer doormats. But in the seventh inning at Yankee Stadium on Tuesday night, Jeter ranged far to his right for a dazzling play that preserved Pettitte's shutout and punctuated the Yankees' 5-0 victory.

Jeter drove in the first two runs with a third-inning double off an overpowering Scott Kazmir. He later singled and scored in the eighth inning, but the defensive highlight seemed at least as satisfying, considering the criticism Jeter takes for his defense.

"I guess you've got to ask the people that criticize me; maybe they'll write a different story," Jeter said. "Send 'em a tape."

Willy Aybar batted with two out and runners at the corners, pulling a hard grounder past third baseman Alex Rodriguez and onto the grass in shallow left field. Jeter dashed over, took about five steps into the outfield and fired a jump throw across his body to cut down the runner at second.

It is a play Jeter has made many times — balls to his left are harder to reach — but Manager Joe Girardi said he did not expect it this time. To Girardi, executing the throw made the play stand out.

"I just think the control — that he's able to jump and spin and make the throw right on the money," Girardi said. "That's impressive to me."

Tyler Kepner

A Sampling of Regular Season Game Highlights

YANKEES 12, WHITE SOX 1, *June 11, 1997*
Jeter scored three of the Yankees' first five runs while reaching base in four straight at-bats to help ignite four damaging rallies.

ANGELS 4, YANKEES 2, *June 21, 1999*
In the third inning, the Angels' Randy Velarde broke his bat swinging at a pitch and hit a looper toward left field, where Chad Curtis got a late jump. But Jeter, running full speed and looking over his head, caught the ball some 90 to 100 feet into left field, with his glove outstretched and his back to home plate.

Darin Erstad, the Anaheim base runner at second, was so sure the ball would fall that he had rounded third, and after Jeter made his catch, he whirled and fired to second to complete the double play. Joe Torre, who managed Ozzie Smith in St. Louis, said: "I don't remember a better play by a shortstop, going out that far."

YANKEES 7, INDIANS 4, *July 20, 2003*
Nearly 55,000 people stood to see what would happen with a full count, the bases loaded and two outs. Jason Giambi slapped the ball up the middle, and his three-run single in the fifth inning lifted the Yankees over Cleveland. Yes, really: a three-run single. Derek Jeter, who had just lashed a run-scoring single, got such a huge jump that he was at second by the time the Indians' C. C. Sabathia threw the pitch. Jeter scored behind John Flaherty and Alfonso Soriano.

"I take a lot of pride in running the bases," Jeter said. When asked later if he could recall the last time he scored from first base on a single, Jeter said: "I have no idea. Little League, maybe."

YANKEES 6, RANGERS 2, *Aug. 6, 2003*
Derek Jeter smoked homers to right in his first two at-bats, and he followed them with a deep fly that Ramon Nivar caught at the warning track. Jeter's two-homer game was his first in two years. "It's not often my name's in the middle of a power display," he said.

Jeter has never hit three homers in a game, but he seems capable of almost anything now. After separating his shoulder on opening night, Jeter was sluggish when he returned. As recently as June 18, his average was .247. Since then, he is batting .401 and looking better than he has in years.

YANKEES 11, METS 8, *June 17, 2007*
Derek Jeter was the most valuable player when the Yankees beat the Mets in the 2000 World Series, and he has never stopped torturing the team across town. Of all the players who have batted at least 200 times against the Mets, Jeter has the best batting average.

The Yankees overcame three deficits in the early innings yesterday, and Jeter put them ahead for good with a two-run homer. The fourth-inning homer was the second of four hits for Jeter, whose .383 career average against the Mets leads all hitters, according to the Elias Sports Bureau.

YANKEES 10, WHITE SOX 0, *Aug. 30, 2009*
Derek Jeter was hitting .443 in his last 16 games, but that did not stop him from bunting with runners on first and second and no outs in the second. After Jeter's sacrifice moved the runners ahead, Johnny Damon hit a two-run double.

Although Jeter's bunt helped push a 2-0 lead to 4-0, it was a curious choice by one of the American League's best hitters. "It was the right thing to do," he said. Jeter was trying to bunt for a hit; the backup plan was to at least put two men in scoring position. When Jeter was asked about the value of hitting, not bunting, to advance runners, he dismissed the notion. "I really don't care who knocks them in, man," he said.

Jeter and Teixeira Receive Gold Glove Awards

Nov. 11, 2009 | Derek Jeter, whose defense has been criticized in recent years through statistical analyses, won a Gold Glove award for his defense, joining Yankees teammate Mark Teixeira on the list of American League recipients released Tuesday. No other team had multiple winners.

At 35, Jeter became the second-oldest shortstop to win the award; Luis Aparicio won it at 36 in 1970. Jeter has won four Gold Gloves, collecting the others from 2004 to 2006.

Although Jeter's defense had come under scrutiny in some statistical analyses, the opposing managers and coaches who voted on the award clearly did not see any decline. Jeter made 8 errors in 554 chances, a .986 fielding percentage.

David Waldstein

White Sox Take Lead; Jeter Takes It Back

May 1, 2010 | When the Yankees have a number of regulars struggling, as they currently do, they can usually depend on a timely performance from their captain, Derek Jeter.

Jeter had a two-run home run in the fifth inning and a two-run triple in the seventh Friday night as the Yankees opened a homestand against the Chicago White Sox with a 6-4 victory.

Jeter also singled and scored in the first. And in the eighth, he scooted to his left for a ground ball, steadied himself and threw out Mark Kotsay in what might have been the game's defensive highlight.

Or perhaps the defensive highlight came in the fifth, when Jeter fielded a ground ball, caught Gordon Beckham in a base-running mistake and started a rundown that ended with Jeter's tagging out Beckham.

Starter Andy Pettitte, who went six innings, focused on Jeter's hitting.

"Oh, man," Pettitte said. "Anybody ask me who you want up at the plate, in all the years I've played, he's the man. He loves it. You can see it in his eyes. He embraces the situation."

Joe Lapointe

In chilly, windy, wet weather, Jeter gets ready to drive in the last run of a rain-shortened 5-1 Yankees victory over the Texas Rangers at Yankee Stadium, *April 16, 2010.* Photo: Jim McIsaac, Getty Images

Derek Jeter is awarded
first base, if not an
Emmy, after a pitch hits
his bat — but not any part
of his body.
Photo: Chris O'Meara,
Associated Press

> "Next time somebody steals a base and a guy doesn't tag you, and the umpire calls you out, do you want the fielder to say, 'No, sir, I didn't tag him, so let's just keep him here?' Come on."

DEREK JETER, *Sept. 18, 2010*

Jeter Stars in Phantom (Hit) of the Ballpark

Sept. 16, 2010 | Derek Jeter reached first base in the pivotal seventh inning Wednesday night without actually getting plunked. Karma, however, works in strange ways.

After Jeter's phantom hit-by-pitch immediately preceded a go-ahead homer by Curtis Granderson in the top of the seventh, the Tampa Bay Rays' Dan Johnson clobbered his second two-run homer of the night in the bottom of the inning, which negated Jeter's contentious play.

Jeter is so respected that he is usually cheered, even in opposing ballparks. But when he was in the on-deck circle as an eighth-inning rally fizzled, fans at Tropicana Field in St. Petersburg, Fla., chanted, "Jeter cheater!"

An inning earlier, Rays Manager Joe Maddon was ejected after arguing that a pitch from Chad Qualls hit the knob of Jeter's bat, bouncing into fair territory, and not his left forearm. Asked where the ball hit, Jeter smiled.

"The bat," he said. And nowhere else? "Well, I mean, they told me to go to first," he said.

Jeter sold the play well. The bat flew out of his hands, and he jumped away as the trainer Gene Monahan came out.

"Vibration," Jeter said. "And acting."

The umpires convened, upholding the original call. Stunned, Maddon kept arguing. Perhaps softened by a sweet 4-3 victory, after the game Maddon called it a heady play.

"If our guys did it, I would have applauded that, too," Maddon said. "It's a great performance on his part."

Ben Shpigel

Analysis: Reviews Are In on Jeter's Role

Sept. 19, 2010 | Jeter may be Sports Illustrated's reigning "Sportsman of the Year," but he will do almost anything to win. On Wednesday, that approach steered him toward the boundaries of baseball's unwritten rules without actually going beyond them.

That code allows players to sell phantom tags to umpires or to make believe a ball that was trapped was actually caught. It allows a catcher to try to trick an umpire into calling a ball a strike. And, in the case of Jeter, who represented the tying run, it allows a player to pretend that a pitch hit him.

Those who make their living in baseball just shrugged.

"I cannot understand what the commotion is," said the Fox baseball broadcaster Tim McCarver, a former major league catcher. "I can't believe anyone would say that's cheating."

McCarver lauded Jeter's awareness of what was at stake. "What upset some people, perhaps, is that he was so demonstrative when it hit the bat, but to think that quickly is remarkable," he said.

Keith Hernandez, the Mets broadcaster and former first baseman, said he would have "no issue whatsoever" if someone reached base on a phantom hit-by-pitch.

Would he say anything to the player? "I would call him Laurence Olivier and say, 'Good one,'" Hernandez said.

Ben Shpigel, with David Waldstein, Richard Sandomir and Tyler Kepner

"Your goal going into the season is to win the championship. Our goal isn't, 'Let's make the playoffs this year, or let's win the A.L. pennant.' If you don't win a championship, then the season is a failure."

DEREK JETER, *Oct. 14, 2001*

A pumped-up Derek Jeter is the first to take the field at Yankee Stadium for the deciding Game 6 of the 2009 World Series against the Philadelphia Phillies, *Nov. 9, 2009.*
Photo: Barton Silverman, The New York Times

CHAPTER **4**

POSTSEASONS

Derek Jeter's postseason career mirrored his professional career: he started off slowly but quickly figured things out. In the first at-bat of his first playoff game, against Texas in the 1996 American League Division Series, Jeter struck out in a Yankees loss. By the next day, he had three hits and was well on his way to his first of several postseason series batting .350 or better.

The Yankees won the World Series that October [see p. 37], and did it again in 1998, 1999 and 2000. The last of those triumphs came in the first subway World Series since 1956, and it was fitting that Jeter, by then the prince of New York baseball, was named Most Valuable Player for hitting .409.

By the time the Yankees won another World Series, in 2009, they were playing in a new stadium, with a new manager and a new collection of stars. But Jeter was still the team's centerpiece, and he hit .407 in a six-game victory over the Phillies.

Jeter's body of postseason work closely resembles his production in the regular season. That reflects a natural balancing of statistics over time, but it also confirms that Jeter is the same player against the best competition, at the most heightened moments, as he is across the grind of 162 games.

It should be no surprise, of course, that the postseason stage does not rattle Jeter. In 1999, when he was 25 years old, Jeter waited on deck during a World Series game the Yankees were losing in Atlanta. Spotting a familiar spectator in the front row, Jeter posed a one-word question: "Nervous?"

The fan was George Steinbrenner. The Yankees went on to sweep the Series.

For 35th Time, Yankees Reach the World Series

Oct. 14, 1998 | The Yankees won the American League championship last night with a 9-5 victory over the Cleveland Indians in Game 6.

Before 57,142 fans at Yankee Stadium, Scott Brosius hit a three-run home run, Derek Jeter stroked a two-run triple and Ramiro Mendoza and Mariano Rivera pitched flawless relief in a game in which the Yankees nearly blew a 6-0 lead.

When the players were damp and covered with Champagne, Jeter spotted a head of perfectly coiffed gray hair in the middle of the Yankees' clubhouse.

"Hold on," Jeter yelled out. "Hold on. Somebody's dry around here."

And with that, he reached and emptied a bottle of bubbly over the Yankees' principal owner, George Steinbrenner, who flinched and laughed.

"I got him," Jeter said, escaping.

Buster Olney

▲ Jeter hugs Luis Sojo (19) as Jorge Posada (20) and other Yankees celebrate winning the American League championship.
Photo: G. Paul Burnett, The New York Times

► Yankees and San Diego Padres players stand for the National Anthem, between their introductions and the start of Game 1 of the World Series at Yankee Stadium, *Oct. 17, 1998.*
Photo: Doug Pensinger, Allsport

Yanks Sweep Series and Assure Legacy

Oct. 22, 1998 | The Yankees have been a team greater than the sum of its parts all year, and when they secured their own corridor in history tonight, it was appropriate that a pitcher who had struggled in recent weeks pushed them over the finish line.

Andy Pettitte, dropped to the back of the Yankees' rotation for the World Series, applied the final piece to their mosaic tonight, pitching seven and a third shutout innings in San Diego and outdueling Kevin Brown in a 3-0 victory over the San Diego Padres in Game 4. In achieving their first Series sweep since 1950 and seventh in their history, the Yankees wrapped up their 24th championship and the second in the last three years.

The Yankees set an American League record with 114 victories in the regular season, then eliminated Texas, three games to none, Cleveland, 4-2, and San Diego, 4-0. The Yankees finished the year with 125 victories and 50 losses in the regular season and postseason combined, shattering the previous record of 118. Their winning percentage of .714 is the third best in history for World Series winners, behind the 1927 Yankees (.722) and the 1909 Pittsburgh Pirates (.717).

The Yankees will be toasted by New York for the second time in three years in a parade through lower Manhattan Friday morning.

Scott Brosius, named the most valuable player in the Series, sensed as the ninth inning began that he would make the final play, and so it was: The Padres pinch-hitter Mark Sweeney grounded to third base, and after Brosius threw to first for the

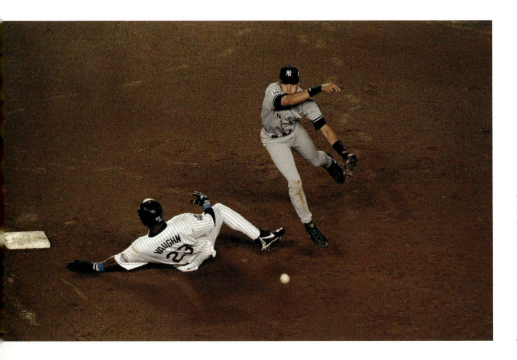

After getting the force-out on the Padres' Greg Vaughn, Jeter completes the double play against Ken Caminiti in the sixth inning of Game 4 at Qualcomm Stadium in San Diego, *Oct. 21, 1998. Photo: Vincent Laforet, Allsport*

Yankees pile on top of
Mariano Rivera to
celebrate their sweep of
the World Series.
*Photo: Chang W. Lee,
The New York Times*

final out, he raised his hands into the air. Mariano Rivera, the Yankees' closer, dropped to his knees near the mound, and the other Yankees embraced and piled around him.

"This is as good as any team I've ever had," said the Yankees' principal owner, George Steinbrenner, his hair slick from Champagne. "This is as good as any team that's ever played the game."

Said right fielder Paul O'Neill, a member of the 1990 Cincinnati Reds, the last team to have swept the World Series: "This is a special team. The things we accomplished won't be done for a long time."

Players gathered in the clubhouse to hoist Champagne bottles and chant the name of Darryl Strawberry, who is recovering at his New Jersey home following the removal of a cancerous tumor. Then they called out Brosius' name, but he was in the family room, to spend time with his family, including his father, who is being treated for cancer.

The Yankees broke through in the sixth, with one out. Derek Jeter hit a high bouncer toward shortstop and, running hard all the way as he always does, easily beat the throw from Chris Gomez. O'Neill, his World Series batting average hovering barely above .100, turned on a low fastball and pulled it into the right-field corner, the ball skidding on the hard outfield surface and reaching the wall. Jeter raced around second, turned at third and stopped, while O'Neill rambled into second base.

Bernie Williams swung fully and bounced a high chopper off the plate, the ball caroming high into the air, toward the pitcher's mound; moving on contact, Jeter broke from third. Brown glanced homeward, but Jeter was already knocking catcher Carlos Hernandez off his feet with a slide across home, and the San Diego ace had to settle for an out at first. The Yankees scored 965 runs in the regular season and another 59 in their first 12 games of the postseason.

The Yankees added two runs in the top of the eighth against Brown on two walks and two hits. The Yankees then had to survive one last scare in the bottom of the eighth. Pettitte walked Quilvio Veras and allowed a single to Tony Gwynn with one out, and the crowd of 65,427 — the largest ever to see a baseball game in this city — screamed together, hoping for comeback. Jeff Nelson relieved Pettitte and whiffed Greg Vaughn, but when he fell behind Ken Caminiti, two balls and no strikes, Torre called for Rivera.

Caminiti lined a single to right field, loading the bases for Jim Leyritz, the former Yankee with a penchant for postseason home runs. But Leyritz lined out to Williams.

Later, Jeter's shirt and face were wet from Champagne; a bottle in one hand and a cigar in the other. "I'm a little young to know about the teams back in the early 1900's," said the 24-year-old Jeter, "but we were 125 and 50, and there's not too many teams that can say that."

Just one.

Buster Olney

Just Sit Back and Enjoy the Show at Shortstop

Oct. 14, 1999 | Nomar leaped to steal a hit from the Yankees, then Derek leaped to swipe one back from the Red Sox, so Nomar leaped even higher to pilfer another. Derek made a sweet play in the shortstop hole, but then bounced the throw to second base for an error. Then Nomar made an even sweeter play in shallow left field, but unintentionally mimicked Derek by bouncing his throw to second.

The game was only three innings old, but the intense matchup between the Yankees and the Red Sox already featured a marvelous duel between the dazzling shortstops whose surnames are not necessary. Derek versus Nomar, Nomar against Derek.

Obviously, the game eventually overtook the story of the two shortstops. Garciaparra and Jeter are terrific, but neither wound up being involved in the final run in the 10th inning because Bernie Williams ripped a homer off Rod Beck that soared over the center-field fence and catapulted the Yankees to a dramatic 4-3 victory over the Red Sox.

But the 57,181 fans at Yankee Stadium when Game 1 of the American League Championship Series began last night were gawking at every move Jeter and Garciaparra made by the second inning.

It was intriguing to watch the shortstops play a game within the game and exciting to watch them fuel the debate about who is better. After the gorgeous plays that Jeter and Garciaparra made, the question should be answered with another question. Who is better? Who cares? Just enjoy the show.

The rivalry between the Yankees and the Red Sox will always be intense because they have a legendary history, because they are in the American League East and because, for the next decade, it should continue to be enhanced by Jeter and Garciaparra. Just as it was last night when Jeter and Garciaparra combined for three errors and still managed to put on a terrific defensive display.

"Whenever I hear my name in the same sentence as his, I think that's an honor," Garciaparra said. "I think he's absolutely tremendous."

Jeter, who also had two hits and one run batted in to Garciaparra's 0 for 4 night, said, "It seemed like that," when asked if he and Garciaparra had a personal duel going on. "He mentioned something to me when I was on second base. He's a great player."

This is the way Yankees-Red Sox should be.

Jack Curry

Yankees owner George Steinbrenner and Jeter wear new caps marking the team's second straight American League pennant, thanks to a 6-1 Game 5 victory over the Boston Red Sox at Fenway Park, *Oct. 18, 1999. Photo: Matt York, Agence France-Presse/Getty Images*

Jeter douses Manager
Joe Torre with
Champagne after
the Yankees' sweep of
the Atlanta Braves in
the World Series.
*Photo: Barton Silverman,
The New York Times*

Yankees Sweep Braves for 25th Title

Oct. 28, 1999 | Roger Clemens was traded to the Yankees on the first day of spring training, and on the last day of the World Series he became a Yankee. Clemens shut out the Atlanta Braves into the eighth inning last night and the Yankees went on to win, 4-1, at Yankee Stadium, clinching a four-game sweep, the Yankees' 25th championship of the century and their third title in four years.

The Yankees' victory was their 12th consecutive in the World Series, tying a record. Mariano Rivera was named the most valuable player after three scoreless appearances in relief.

Rivera threw the last pitch of the Series in the bottom of the ninth inning, and when Keith Lockhart popped a fly ball to left field, Rivera stood and stared, emotionless, watching left fielder Chad Curtis settle under the ball and make the catch.

And then they went crazy. Rivera raised his arms, turned and embraced catcher Jorge Posada, and third baseman Scott Brosius joined them. They all gathered in a circle behind the mound, while security officials and mounted police officers began rushing onto the field. Clemens, jacketed, ran onto the field, arms raised. Paul O'Neill, who only hours earlier had learned in an early-morning phone call that his father, Charles O'Neill, had died, was the last of the position players to join the happy scrum.

They began trading hugs, Manager Joe Torre joining, and it was in those moments, some of them said later, that the gravity of all they endured this year began to hit them. Brosius's father had died, and so had the father of the infielder Luis Sojo, and Torre was found to have prostate cancer. They had worn the No. 5 in a black sphere on one shoulder, after Joe DiMaggio died in March, and late in the season, a black armband was added following the death of the Hall of Fame pitcher Catfish Hunter. "We're all family here," Brosius said.

As O'Neill traded embraces, he burst into tears, and with his head down, he rushed off the field, seeking seclusion. His teammates gathered in the Yankees' clubhouse to spray champagne — Derek Jeter doused the principal owner, George Steinbrenner — and share their joy.

Just before Clemens scaled the mound to start the game, Brosius handed him the baseball. Then Jeter jogged in, with his perpetual half-grin, and said: "This is what you've worked for, this is what you've been wanting for so long. Now go out there and get it done," and with that, he slapped Clemens on the backside with his glove.

Chuck Knoblauch reached first on an infield single to lead off the third, and Jeter spanked a broken-bat single to right, Knoblauch sprinting to third and pulling into the base standing. Manager Bobby Cox could be seen shaking his head slightly; there was no score, but it felt as if the conclusion was foregone.

O'Neill struck out, with Jeter stealing second, and the Braves intentionally walked Bernie Williams. Bases loaded, one out. Tino Martinez then turned on a fastball, pulling it toward first base, the ball hit hard. Ryan Klesko, the Atlanta first baseman, waved his glove at the ball, which bounded off his wrist and rolled into short right field. Knoblauch scored and Jeter followed, taking the last steps toward home plate with his right fist raised. Two batters later, Posada stroked a single to right, and Williams rambled homeward safely. The Yankees' lead was three runs.

Buster Olney

Jeter, Mariano Rivera and
Jorge Posada celebrate
the Yankees' 9-7 Game 6
victory over the Seattle
Mariners to clinch the
American League cham-
pionship for the third
straight year, *Oct. 18, 2000.*
*Photo: Vincent Laforet, The
New York Times*

> "We won 114 games in '98 and we won 87 this year and we're starting out 0-0 both times. There are 22 teams out there who wish they could be where we are."

DEREK JETER on the Yankees' getting into the playoffs despite a mediocre regular season, *Oct. 3, 2000*

> "People want to write us off. But until somebody beats us, we're the champions."

DEREK JETER after the Yankees' hard-fought, five-game victory over the widely favored Oakland Athletics in the A.L. Division Series, *Oct. 10, 2000*

Jeter Pays Price in Off-Season, Seattle Pays Price in Postseason

Oct. 15, 2000 | The alarm clock buzzes at 8 a.m. in January, and Derek Jeter crawls out of bed to start another day of workouts. Spring training is six weeks away, but Jeter is already working because he wants to be able to do exactly what he did last night.

Jeter wants to get stronger, better and smarter, which is why he moved to Tampa, Fla., six years ago and spends 50 weeks a year playing baseball. His eyes are still bleary and the weather is cool when Jeter gets to the Yankees' minor league complex there. The fields are empty and Jeter starts to work like an unemployed minor leaguer.

The relevance of those wake-up calls resonated in Game 4 of the American League Championship Series last night. Jeter knows the lusty swing that produced a prodigious three-run homer off Paul Abbott and helped steer Roger Clemens and the Yankees past the fading Mariners, 5-0, was born in a backyard in Kalamazoo, Mich., and is now bred in Tampa.

As Jeter's shot kept climbing to center field, Mike Cameron kept pursuing it. The acrobatic Cameron stole a homer from Jeter in April, but his leap was in vain this time. When Abbott saw Jeter's ball vanish over the fence, he said, "Oh my God." There was silence at Safeco Field in Seattle when Jeter, blowing a bubble and pumping his fist, breezed around the bases.

"Huge at-bat, huge hit," right fielder Paul O'Neill said. "He's Derek Jeter, man. That's what he's supposed to do."

Because Clemens was intimidating the Mariners, Jeter's homer in the fifth inning surely deflated them. The game was over. Clemens buzzed fastballs that reached 99 miles an hour

and he was even more relaxed after Jeter's homer, finishing with a one-hitter spiced with 15 strikeouts.

After hitting 15 homers this season, his lowest total since he had 10 in 1997, Jeter has already belted two during the A.L.C.S. Jeter hit a two-run homer during the seven-run eighth inning in Game 2 and then helped bury the Mariners last night and probably forever.

Back in Wesley Chapel, Fla., Gary Denbo was smiling. Denbo, who was Jeter's first minor league manager and is now the Yankees' hitting coordinator, works with him during all of those quiet mornings on barren fields.

Denbo called Jeter last week and offered three pieces of advice. He told Jeter that he needed to stand more upright because he had no chance to bash certain inside pitches if he tilted forward. Denbo also advised Jeter to try to hit to the middle of the field instead of trying to pull everything. Finally, Denbo counseled Jeter on taking a better swing path and moving his bat through the strike zone at a steady rate. On the memorable homer, Jeter remained upright, he hit the ball to the middle of the field and his swing was true.

"It's a good feeling to know that you've worked with him and maybe you've contributed a little bit to his success," Denbo said by telephone last night. "He's a great student. After you talk to him, he does it."

When Jeter was asked if he might buy Denbo dinner, he said, "I owe him a lot more than one dinner."

Jack Curry

Subway Series: Jeter Takes Out Shea Fans Right Off

Oct. 26, 2000 | Shea Stadium was buzzing in the afterglow of the Mets' first victory of the World Series on Tuesday night when Derek Jeter was introduced as the leadoff hitter for the Yankees last night. Jeter was oblivious to the rowdy energy around him.

Whether Jeter was responding to Joe Torre's clairvoyant hunch to change the lineup, the Yankees' shortstop slipped the Mets' fans in the crowd a sedative the instant he lifted a fastball by Bobby J. Jones over the wall on the first pitch in Game 4 of the World Series.

Jeter set the tone of the game, changed the mood of the stadium and gave the Yankees the critical first run. Nine innings later, it was still as important as it was when it left Jeter's bat in a managerial tug of war the Yankees won, 3-2, to take a commanding three-games-to-one lead in the World Series.

"Everyone seems to ask if I'm changing my approach when I'm the leadoff hitter," said Jeter. "But I'm aggressive, and I've been known to swing at the first pitch. With runs tough to come by in the postseason, you want to score early."

eeking a first punch into the Mets' spirits, Torre removed Jose Vizcaino from the top spot and used Jeter there for the first time in the Series.

"We've won some games with Jeter in the No. 1 hole," Torre said before the game. "He's just batted second more than any other position. If I recollect correctly, in the five years he's been here, he's batted everywhere from first to ninth. It doesn't matter to him. I'd like to see him score a run in the first inning."

Torre's wishes were answered swiftly.

Jeter did not stop at one moment, though. In his next at-bat, he unearthed enough speed to turn a double into a triple and went on to score his second run of the game — his fifth of the World Series.

Selena Roberts

"He's allowed."

GEORGE STEINBRENNER on being drenched with Champagne by Derek Jeter, during the Yankees' clubhouse celebration of their third world championship in a row, *Oct. 27, 2000*

Jeter, the M.V.P., Says This Title Is Most Gratifying

Oct. 27, 2000 | With a home run in each of the last two games and a .409 batting average, Yankee shortstop Derek Jeter was named the most valuable player of the Subway Series last night, but he deferred the honor.

"You could've picked a name out of the hat; we have 25 M.V.P.'s," he said. "First game, Vizcaino. What O'Neill's done, our pitching staff, our bullpen, Luis Sojo. You don't rely on one guy."

His cap on backward, Jeter, 26, was wearing a gray World Series champions sweatshirt that was wet with Champagne spray.

"This is by far the best team we've played," he said, meaning the Mets as a World Series opponent. "All the games could've gone either way. Every year is a different story, but I'd be lying if I said this wasn't more gratifying. Oakland was the hottest team when we played 'em, Seattle was tough, and the Mets were the best team I've seen in five years."

In his five seasons, Jeter has earned four World Series rings, including one in each of the last three years.

For the Subway Series, he had 9 hits in 22 at-bats, including two doubles, a triple and two homers. His first-pitch homer set the tone for the Yankees' 3-2 victory in Game 4 and his one-out homer off Al Leiter created a 2-2 tie in the sixth inning of last night's 4-2 victory.

The homers sparked his .864 slugging average. He also walked three times. Jeter's 19 total bases set a five-game Series record. He tied five-game records with his nine hits and six runs scored.

Asked what his reaction would be if Joe Torre were to retire as manager, he smiled.

"If he retires, I'm going to retire," Jeter said. "He continues to push the right buttons. He's got a magic wand. You can't say enough about him as a manager. He's a player's manager. He lets you play. He doesn't get on you unless you make mental mistakes. He has a lot of confidence in everybody."

Dave Anderson

A City's Rite of Autumn: Yankee Fans Paint the Town in Pinstripes Again

Oct. 31, 2000 | Once again, the city all but carried them on its shoulders up Broadway yesterday, as police officers parted the crush of their admirers and sanitation workers swept debris from their path. And once again, hundreds of thousands of people took off from work and school to jam Lower Manhattan, throw fists of confetti and holler themselves hoarse, all in their honor.

They are neither war heroes nor astronauts; they are simply baseball players. But within their narrow, highly specialized field, the New York Yankees proved they are among the best teams in sports history last week by winning their fourth World Series in five years. And for the fourth time in five years, the city threw the Yankees a parade that was equal parts joyous, idolatrous and corny. Only this time, even more so.

That is because the vanquished of past Series came from Atlanta and San Diego, cities that do little more than annoy Yankee fans. This year, their Yankees beat the other New York team, the Mets — a fact that seemed to heighten the pitch of the primal, plaintive cry that echoed down Broadway: "Let's Go Yankees!"

Then came another float, with the crowd-pleasing shortstop Derek Jeter.

"Derek Jeter saw me!" said Mary O'Regan, a 15-year-old girl from Brooklyn whose face was painted blue and white with the Yankee logo. "He saw me and he smiled. I'm so excited."

Dan Barry

Jorge Posada reaches for the ball flipped by an out-of-position Jeter in time for the crucial out at the plate.
Photo: Chang W. Lee, The New York Times

New Mr. October Polishes His Growing Luster, and Keeps Yankees Alive

Oct. 14, 2001 | Reggie Jackson is synonymous with excellence during the month of October, so much so that his nickname was Mr. October. Jackson offers compliments about players about as often as he answers to Mr. September, but Jackson gushed about Derek Jeter tonight.

Jeter is only 27, but he added to his postseason legacy with an amazing defensive play tonight in Oakland, Calif., that helped prevent a run and helped save the Yankees as they edged the Oakland Athletics, 1-0, in Game 3 of the division series.

"He's a big-time player," Jackson said. "He makes great plays. Great player." Jackson kept repeating that phrase.

Terrence Long had ripped a two-out shot into the right-field corner and Jeremy Giambi was chugging around third base with the potential tying run. Jeter noticed that Shane Spencer's throw was about to sail over two cutoff men, second baseman Alfonso Soriano and first baseman Tino Martinez, and was heading toward a perilous empty spot between first base and the plate.

Jeter, who is supposed to be stationed on the mound so he can throw to third or home, swooped in to collect the ball about 20 feet from the plate. He caught the ball but had no time to turn his body toward the plate. Instead, Jeter shoveled the ball to catcher Jorge Posada like an option quarterback running

the wishbone. Posada caught the flip and tagged Giambi on the left leg. Giambi did not slide and was out. Jeter pumped his fist. The Yankees exhaled.

"I didn't have time to turn around and set up and throw," Jeter said. "Basically, I just got rid of it. If I tried to spin around, he would have been safe."

General Manager Brian Cashman compared Jeter to Superman, faster than an errant cutoff throw, able to catch a loose ball and, with his body moving in one direction, throw in the other direction to prevent the A's from scoring a precious run. Jeter kept saying he was simply doing his job, but he was being modest.

"Thank God Jete was there," said Spencer, who added that he muttered a profanity after the throw soared past both cutoff men.

Mike Mussina pitched seven scoreless innings tonight, Posada provided a monstrous homer and Jeter, a little Mr. October, made a superb play that enabled the Yankees to play for at least one more October day.

Jack Curry

What Can We Do Next? Just Watch Jeter Play

Oct. 17, 2001 | We know the score, the season and the shortstop. We see the stadium, standing room only. We feel the pressure and we are sure he must feel it, too. Derek Jeter of the Yankees stands in the middle of all we see and he spends a good portion of his day making faces. He grins, he smiles, he smirks. He catches the eye of third baseman Scott Brosius and laughs, he jokes with a base runner. If a ball is hit his way, well, he will catch it. He knows that.

We see a pitcher and we know his portfolio. Jeter sometimes does not know the pitcher's name. All he wants to know is how hard he is throwing, information he gets with a glance to a radar gun operator behind home plate. "He's got nothing," Jeter sometimes announces after returning to the dugout.

We see a complicated situation fraught with consequence. He sees a bouncing ball that needs to be retrieved and relayed. After Jeter improvised on the pivotal play in Game 3 of the division series in Oakland last week, he said, "It's my job to make a play," as if he were saying "it's my job to empty the dishwasher and take out the trash."

We have come to expect great plays from Jeter every year, and every year his great plays surprise us, a trait common in Babe Ruth, Lou Gehrig, Joe DiMaggio and Mickey Mantle. It wasn't an accident that the Yankees gave him a single-digit number.

Jeter is uniformly polite. He does not boast. But he is not modest. "Are you kidding?" Luis Sojo said last spring, laughing. Jeter, Sojo said, doesn't just think he's going to kick your backside, "he knows it."

Jeter did not have a great season, relative to the standards he has established. He was a borderline All-Star candidate this year, and in the weeks leading up to the game, ESPN promoted his inclusion as if it were a fait accompli. "Are you comfortable with that?" a reporter asked Jeter, clearly bothering the shortstop.

Manager Joe Torre named him to the team the next day. "I guess that answers your question," Jeter said to the reporter, a rebuke with a smile.

Jeter's face is everywhere: commercials, public service advertising, book covers, magazine covers. He sits through elaborate photo sessions under the direction of accomplished professionals. He turns his head in the on-deck circle for a 10-year-old with a disposable camera.

Hal Newhouser, the most valuable player of the American League in 1944 and 1945, scouted Jeter in high school and saw the confidence in all he did. This young man will help his team win championships for many years, Newhouser reported to the Houston Astros, and when the Astros decided to take someone else, Newhouser quit his job.

Jeter, now 27, hit a home run in his first game as the Yankees' everyday shortstop in 1996. He hit a game-tying home run — the Jeffrey Maier home run — in the first game of a playoff series against Baltimore that year. He got at least one hit in 14 consecutive World Series games. He slugged a home run on the first pitch of Game 4 of the 2000 World Series, in Shea Stadium, and hit a home run the next day, as well. He's been the most valuable player in an All-Star Game and in a World Series. His batting average had risen in each level of the postseason going into this year's playoffs: .312 average in the first round, .319 in the second round, .342 in the World Series.

"You have to enjoy being in those situations," Jeter said the other night. "It doesn't mean you're going to be successful every time. It doesn't mean you're going to make every play. You're still going to make errors. You're going to make mistakes. You just don't shy away from it."

The Yankees had a runner at third with one out in Game 5 on Monday night, and the Oakland infielders moved in and shifted a little to the right, anticipating Jeter would hit the ball to the right side, as he does most of the time. Jeter checked on the velocity of the pitcher's fastball, strolled to the batter's box.

"If it's a pitch I think I can hit, I'm going to swing," Jeter once said, detailing his philosophy on hitting. So with Oakland's infield in and needing a fly ball, he abandoned his inside-out swing, pulled the ball and drove the first pitch deep into left field, driving home a run.

Later in the game, in the tense eighth inning, a foul ball drifted toward the stands, and Jeter raced over from shortstop. There was not enough room for him to make a catch, we thought.

And then Jeter leapt into the stands to backhand the ball, his spikes nearly clipping Brosius in the face.

"Derek, from 1996 when I first met the young man, has that look in his eye," Torre said afterward. "It's a look that you don't teach. It's a look that you have, that fire in your belly, that love for competition. This kid, with that play the other day, thinks cool in hot situations. He never had regard for putting his body in peril, or looking bad with a bad swing. We have many of them, but he's a true leader at a very early age."

We know the score, the season and the shortstop. We feel the pressure and we are sure he must feel it, too. Derek Jeter just plays.

Buster Olney

Uncomplaining but still battered days after a tumble into the stands while catching a foul pop-up in the division series, Jeter ices his sore right shoulder — among other ailments — following Game 2 of the championship series against Seattle, *Oct. 18, 2001.*
Photo: Barton Silverman,
The New York Times

"You listen to some people say baseball doesn't mean anything to the city. Baseball's not going to heal the world, it's not going to heal the city. But if it gives some people something to cheer for, to look forward to, that's what we're here for. Now everyone is looking forward to the World Series."

DEREK JETER on the Yankees' fourth straight A.L. pennant, about six weeks after the 9/11 attacks, *Oct. 24, 2001*

Midnight Thunder in the Bronx

Nov. 1, 2001 | Whenever Babe Ruth and Lou Gehrig hit late-inning home runs to win a Yankee game in that long-ago era of day baseball, it was known as Five O'Clock Lightning.

And last night, Tino Martinez and Derek Jeter produced Midnight Thunder with two of the most theatrical home runs in the Yankees' hallowed World Series history.

With two outs in the ninth inning, the Yankees were down, 3-1, to the Diamondbacks and about to go down by 3-1 in the World Series. But Martinez, the first baseman the Yankees keep hinting they don't want to sign to another contract, hit a towering two-run homer off Byung Hyun Kim over the center-field fence.

In the 10th inning, Jeter, the shortstop who thrives on these moments, sliced a home run into the right-field stands off Kim for a 4-3 victory that squared the Series at 2-2 going into tonight's fifth game.

"I've never hit a walk-off home run before; it was pretty exciting," Jeter said later. "The beauty of the postseason is that it doesn't matter what you've done before because every time you come up, you've got a chance to do something special."

As his teammates pounced on Jeter, a prescient middle-aged fan held up a sign: "Mr. November."

Dave Anderson

"Mr. November" is exultant after hitting his first game-winning home run ever, in Game 4 of the 2001 World Series. *Photo: G. Paul Burnett, The New York Times*

Fearless Angels Leave Yankees Soundly Beaten

Oct. 6, 2002 | In harrowing times this season — this promising season, now emphatically over — people would remind Derek Jeter of the wondrous things the Yankees had accomplished. "Some of us have," Jeter would reply softly.

He was not being snide or self-aggrandizing, merely pointing out that this year's Yankees team was different from last year's Yankees team — considerably so.

Maybe Jeter saw it coming, the 9-5 thumping by the onrushing Anaheim Angels, who outplayed the Yankees for the third straight game and clinched the American League Division Series this afternoon at Edison Field in Anaheim, Calif.

"No team has played better against us," Jeter said graciously, referring to the seven fat years in which he had played shortstop and Joe Torre had managed and the Yankees had won four World Series.

The walloping means there will be no fifth straight pennant that would have tied the major league record.

"We won the first game and they came back in every game," Jeter said, sitting at his locker while Anaheim celebrated winning its first postseason series in the 42 years of the franchise.

The last time the Yankees were stunned like this was in 1995, when Seattle polished them off in its old domed stadium. That defeat cost Buck Showalter his job. The Yankees also lost a first-round series to Cleveland in 1997, but they had not yet become the great American dynasty at the millennium.

Yes, Arizona smoked the Yankees, 15-2, in the sixth game of the World Series last year, then edged them on a flare single off Mariano Rivera in the last inning of a very long season. But that shock came after the Yankees had staged two marvelous rallies in New York.

Jeter smoldered after that Game 7 loss and did not even want to be consoled by Torre. Today Jeter seemed weary and resigned, like a man who had seen it coming.

"A loss is a loss," he said. "The season's a failure."

The Yankees were drastically altered after last year's World Series. Scott Brosius and Paul O'Neill retired, and Tino Martinez and Chuck Knoblauch moved on. That is a lot of change, even for the Yankees.

Hard as it is for fans to accept, even the rich Yankees were not entitled to win. Jeter played today with a stressed right arm and he took a hard foul off his leg, but he managed two singles to give him 101 career hits in the postseason. That is the most in major league history, accomplished, of course, in this age of triple-tier playoffs. But his .500 average for this series was not enough.

In the days to come, George Steinbrenner will surely ponder a purge of this team. How could the Angels, with a payroll of only $77 million, be so much better than his Yankees, with their payroll of $171 million based on his cable riches?

The owner will have plenty of time to ponder and purge. This Yankee team — this very different Yankee team — is now history.

George Vecsey

After singling, Jeter heads to third base at the start of a three-run first-inning rally — but the Angels come back to win, 9-6, the second of three straight victories, *Oct. 4, 2002.* *Photo: Chang W. Lee, The New York Times*

To Understand Success of Jeter, Calm Down

Oct. 7, 2003 | As Derek Jeter flipped a baseball to Alfonso Soriano by the Yankees' dugout last Thursday, he was so calm that he might as well have been wearing shorts and sandals and throwing a Frisbee in Central Park. The Yankees had been heavily scrutinized after a sloppy setback to the Minnesota Twins in the opener of their division series and there were enough negative vibes to cause Manager Joe Torre to conduct a pointed meeting before Game 2.

Jeter gets the force-out at second before leaping to avoid the slide of Doug Mientkiewicz in Game 2 of the division series against the Twins, *Oct. 2, 2003.*
Photo: Barton Silverman, The New York Times

Still, Jeter was relishing the moments leading up to the important game.

"It was just one game," Jeter said. "We'll be fine."

And the Yankees were fine. Because of their superb starting pitching, because of the late-inning pit bull named Mariano Rivera, because of a chunk of offense from Bernie Williams, Hideki Matsui and Jason Giambi and, as usual, because of Jeter's cool, confident play, the Yankees rushed to three straight victories and buried the Twins.

Jeter was not even the best player on his own team during a stellar regular season, but now that the postseason is percolating, he has again climbed to the forefront for the Yankees. He had at least one hit in all four games against the Twins, he reached base 10 times, he batted .429, he hit one homer and he missed another by a foot.

"Jeter is the most relaxed person that I've seen in the postseason," Reggie Jackson, the Hall of Famer, said in a telephone interview. "I would relate him to the way Ron Guidry approached it or Catfish Hunter or Mariano Rivera. There's a relaxed way to go about playing. At the same time, there's tension. You have to be mentally and physically alert. Jeter is always ready."

When Twins Manager Ron Gardenhire was asked if any team could stifle the Yankees, he rambled on about them being the premier team in baseball, he praised Torre and then his mind's Rolodex stopped on J.

"Derek Jeter is as good a player as there is in this league," Gardenhire said. "He leads that baseball team and does a very good job of it."

After coming back from a shoulder injury in the regular season opener, Jeter wound up playing 119 games and hitting .324 with 10 homers and 52 runs batted in. Jeter's defensive skills have eroded and he is slower on grounders to his left. He strikes out a lot and should walk more. He will probably never have the 30-homer season the Yankees once hoped for.

But, when the calendar turns to October, Jeter embraces the enhanced atmosphere and the brighter spotlight. Jeter's 107 postseason hits are a major league record. Jackson, who has advised Jeter about the power of believing — that you are supposed to succeed in pressure situations because you have done it before — said Jeter thrives because he has the talent and because he has the mental makeup to remain placid in precarious spots.

"When you look across the room and you see No. 2 on your team, you know he's going to be ready," Jackson said. "You know he's going to be calm. Everyone sees that and it makes them calm, too. The leader of all of this is Jeter. I put him on a high level as a postseason player."

Jack Curry

Catching a pop-up by Boston's Jason Varitek, Jeter ends Game 5 of the championship series with the Yankees winning 4-2, en route to the pennant, *Oct. 14, 2003.*
Photo: Barton Silverman, The New York Times

Jeter Is Center of Attention, Especially in October

Oct. 23, 2003 | All eyes are on Derek Jeter. Heads turn as he walks through the basement of the ballpark in Miami with giant ice packs on both shoulders.

All eyes are on Derek Jeter, but last night was not one of his finer games. He hit into two double plays as the Yankees lost to the Marlins, 4-3 in 12 innings, to tie the World Series at two games apiece.

The Yankees would not have been here except for Jeter's performance in the seventh game of the American League Championship Series. With the Yankees trailing Pedro Martinez by three runs, Jeter whacked a double off the wall and reached second base and clapped his hands, in joy and in anticipation.

All eyes are on Derek Jeter now that it is October and he is one of two shortstops still playing in North America.

All we heard this past summer was that Derek Jeter had found his level. Limited power. Limited range. And perhaps even slightly passé in the new century of the slugger shortstop.

Ah, yes, we heard those bleats, quite often emanating from Yankees fans themselves, morbidly fearful that somehow a 39th pennant was impossible because Jeter would not slug 40 home runs or steal 40 bases.

Since then, we have seen Tejada pull a rock on the basepaths in the first round. We have seen Nomar blow hot and cold in the A.L.C.S. And here was Derek Jeter, standing on second base, clapping his hands.

All eyes are on Derek Jeter. On Tuesday night, young Josh Beckett blasted through the first 10 Yankees batters. Then Jeter lashed a double into the left-field corner. Once again, in the center of the field, he was the platoon leader waving his hand over his head to signal, "Follow me!" He added two hits and scored three runs.

Last night was a different story. Jeter went 1 for 6 and even made a sloppy tag that did not cost the Yankees. He's not perfect. But the Yankees will count on him as this Series comes down to its final innings.

Jeter has been dominating this team game for eight seasons. He has become a wise old hand, who welcomes the pressure of the World Series, saying, "I grew up with this." He hears the Boss has been quoting Patton or MacArthur or Lombardi about victory once again, and he says, "You know, this is not the first time I have heard this."

Now the World Series will return from the Marlins' stadium to Yankee Stadium. The Yankees will need a serious contribution from Jeter to ward off this low-budget but high-energy team. They will need Jeter standing on second base, clapping his hands, after a big hit.

On Tuesday night, a columnist said to Jeter, "What makes you so cool?" Jeter pointed to his shoulders and told her, "It's the ice."

George Vecsey

Jeter Keeps It Simple: Score Runs, Win

Oct. 8, 2004 | All these years, Derek Jeter has been kidding. There is a statistic that matters to him. A few years ago, Jeter told Luis Sojo that one number drives him.

"The only thing he likes is scoring runs," said Sojo, a former Yankees infielder who now coaches third base. "He doesn't worry about anything else. The one specific number that does inspire him is 100 runs, because he knows that if he scores 100 runs, we have a chance to win 100 games."

It is typical of Jeter, who never complicates a task. The team with the most runs wins, so he may as well try to score.

This single-minded passion fueled Jeter's dash for the plate in the 12th inning on Wednesday at Yankee Stadium. When he slid in safely, he brought the Yankees to Minneapolis for Game 3 of their best-of-five-game division series with the Minnesota Twins tied at one game apiece.

Over his nine-year major league career, his postseason batting average is .313, 2 points lower than his regular-season av-

erage. But every night in the postseason, he seems to have a defining moment.

"He's capable of doing so many things," closer Mariano Rivera said. "He can do it many ways: with the home run, with the steal, with the bunt. He's always there. Always there."

When Jeter stepped in against Brad Radke to lead off the bottom of the first, the Yankees had not scored in 18 postseason innings. Jeter crushed a pitch into the black seats in center field. No Yankee had sent a ball there in the postseason since Reggie Jackson in the 1977 World Series.

"We certainly needed a lift, especially with Minnesota scoring a run in the top of the first," Manager Joe Torre said. "He hit a ball to Reggieland. That's not really part of his signature, but he made a statement there."

In the fifth inning, Jeter fielded a chopper over the middle, stepped on second and fired to first for a double play, erasing the Twins' leadoff base runner. In the seventh, he sacrificed

Miguel Cairo to second so Alex Rodriguez could drive him in with a single.

With one out in the 12th and Cairo on first, Jeter took four straight balls from Joe Nathan, the tiring Twins closer. Rodriguez's double tied the score and moved Jeter to third. Sheffield was walked intentionally.

Sojo approached Jeter during a pitching change and reminded him of the basics.

"I told him, 'Ground ball, we have to go; fly ball, I'll let you know,' " Sojo said. "He said, 'You don't have to let me know anything; I'm going to go no matter what.'"

The Twins moved the outfielders in, and Hideki Matsui ripped a liner to Jacque Jones in right. Jones caught the ball flat-footed and did not anticipate that Jeter would tag up.

"I don't know why," Jeter said. "Probably because he caught it at second base."

Jeter, the Yankees' captain, was undaunted. Instead of breaking for home on the liner, he broke back to third, putting himself in position to tag up. Most runners would be halfway down the base line. Jeter's reaction was pure instinct, and he beat the relay throw.

"That's the way he plays baseball," Cairo said. "His head is into the game from beginning to end, and there's not too many guys that play that way. He never takes his mind off the game."

It is October, and Jeter's mind keeps it simple. Score runs. Keep the other team from scoring. Win the game, always.

"I don't see a better player than that guy in October," Sojo said. "The things that he does, it's unbelievable. Thank God he's on our side."

Tyler Kepner

Jeter Tops Himself

Oct. 4, 2006 | There were others who starred in the Yankees' 8-4 victory over the Detroit Tigers in Game 1 of the A.L. Division Series, but nobody sparkled as brightly as Jeter, who tied a postseason record with five hits.

Jeter, the Yankees' captain, has made a career of rising to meet the moment. This time, he topped himself. Jeter went 5 for 5 and capped his night with a home run over the center-field wall at Yankee Stadium in the eighth inning.

Only five other players have had five hits in a postseason game, including Hideki Matsui in the 2004 American League Championship Series. Jeter singled in the first inning, doubled in the third, singled in the fourth and doubled in the sixth.

Tyler Kepner, with Michael S. Schmidt

Jeter Defends Manager, Hopes He'll Be Back

Oct. 9, 2007 | Derek Jeter's numbers spoke for themselves: a batting average of .176 for the American League Division Series.

But after the Cleveland Indians eliminated Jeter's Yankees with a 6-4 victory last night at Yankee Stadium, Jeter's most pointed words spoke not so much of himself but of his manager, Joe Torre.

"Everyone knows that I love Mr. T.," Jeter said. "He's the best, in my opinion. Hopefully, he is back."

When Jeter was asked to elaborate about the manager he has played for since 1996, Jeter said: "Joe's always the same. That's why he's been successful. Good times, bad times, he's got the perfect mentality for a manager."

Although Torre has won four World Series championships with the Yankees, Jeter said this might have been his best year of managing because he rallied a team that seemed out of the playoffs at midseason.

Jeter looked exhausted after his team was eliminated from the playoffs in the first round for the third consecutive season.

"Last year was frustrating," Jeter said. "The year before that was frustrating. Every year you lose is frustrating. It hurts. It feels bad." Jeter noted how hard it was to win and how the Yankees were the only one of the eight playoff teams to return from 2006.

He finished the series with one run batted in. In postseason play from 1996 through this season, Jeter had batted .370 in the division series, .262 in the League Championship Series and .302 in the World Series.

Joe Lapointe

◄ Jeter leaps up after sliding home for the winning run in the 12th inning of Game 2 of the 2004 division series against the Twins.
Photo: Vincent Laforet, The New York Times

The Phillies' Shane
Victorino watches as
Jeter completes the
eighth-inning double
play on Chase Utley in
Game 2 of the World
Series, *Oct. 29, 2009.*
Photo: Barton Silverman,
The New York Times

Across the Street, It's Still October

Oct. 8, 2009 | The Yankees' old shrine still stands on 161st Street in the Bronx, dark and cold and gutted. The October games that made it so famous have moved across the street, where the new Yankee Stadium hosted its first playoff game in style Wednesday night.

The bright lights twinkled above the signature frieze, and three decks of seats thumped on a night when nearly everything went perfectly for the Yankees. They snuffed the Minnesota Twins, 7-2, in the first game of their division series, benefiting from the kind of shutdown pitching they lacked in October for much of this decade.

The Yankees scripted this after missing the playoffs last season. They signed C. C. Sabathia to be their ace, to overwhelm hitters when he had to. They nurtured and kept homegrown arms like Phil Hughes, Phil Coke and Joba Chamberlain. And they hoped that Mariano Rivera,

as ever, would throttle their opponents. It all happened in Game 1.

Alex Rodriguez shook his playoff slump with two run-scoring singles. Both times, he drove in Derek Jeter, who hit the first postseason homer at the new stadium in the third inning. Casey Stengel, of all people, hit the first across the street, as a New York Giant in the 1923 World Series.

Jeter's homer erased a 2-0 lead the Twins had built in the top of the third against Sabathia. Jeter, who reached base in all four of his at-bats, now has as many postseason homers (18) as Mickey Mantle and Reggie Jackson. That he has done it in many more games does not diminish his reputation.

Tyler Kepner

Exorcising Demons

Oct. 12, 2009 | It took five years of wandering, five years of wild spending and first-round heartbreak and changes both awkward and grand. But the Yankees are back in the American League Championship Series, back where it all went off course in 2004.

They got there by sweeping the Minnesota Twins in the division series with a 4-1 victory in Game 3 on Sunday in Minneapolis.

Mariano Rivera ended the series, saving a victory for Andy Pettitte. But the real save came in the eighth, an inning that started when Nick Punto doubled off Phil Hughes.

Denard Span chopped a ball up the middle, and Derek Jeter corralled it behind second base. Punto said he heard the crowd roar and figured the ball had gone to the outfield. He did not pick up the stop sign from the third-base coach, Scott Ullger, until he had rounded third. Jeter noticed.

"You can't get Span at first," Jeter said. "I saw Punto out of the corner of my eye going home."

Trying to stop his momentum, Punto slid on the artificial turf as Jeter threw home. His stumble gave Jorge Posada enough time to take the throw and fire to Alex Rodriguez for an out that might as well have deflated the Teflon roof.

Tyler Kepner

Jeter's girlfriend, the actress Minka Kelly, helps him celebrate the Yankees' first world championship in nine years.

Photo: Barton Silverman, The New York Times

Jeter looks drained, maybe because he can already envision the end of the Torre era, or because he's about to see Game 2 of the 2007 division series against the Indians go up in a cloud of insects. Bugged by a sudden swarm, reliever Joba Chamberlain gave up the winning run in an eighth inning marked by two walks, a hit batter and two wild pitches.

Photo: Richard Perry, The New York Times

Back on Top, Yankees Add a 27th Title

Nov. 5, 2009 | A sliver of time for other teams is an epoch for the Yankees, who define themselves by championships. For eight seasons, they led the majors in victories, payroll and drama. They built a ballpark, created a network and expanded their brand around the globe. But they did not win the World Series.

Now they have done it. There is a 27th jewel in the Yankees' crown and a peaceful, easy feeling across their empire. The Yankees captured their first title since 2000, humbling the defending champion Philadelphia Phillies on Wednesday, 7-3, in Game 6 of the World Series at Yankee Stadium.

Hideki Matsui homered, with his six runs batted in tying a World Series record, and Andy Pettitte ground through five and two-thirds innings for his second victory in five days. Mariano Rivera collected the final five outs, getting Shane Victorino to ground out to second to end it.

They did it on the eighth anniversary of Rivera's lowest moment, when he blew Game 7 of the 2001 World Series in Arizona. The Yankees lost the World Series again two years later, to Florida, and they did not return until this season, fortifying their roster with free agents around the core of Rivera, Pettitte, Derek Jeter and Jorge Posada.

Pettitte became the second pitcher to win all three clinching games of a postseason. The other was Boston's Derek Lowe in 2004, when the Yankees lost a three-games-to-none lead to the Red Sox, fumbling away a pennant and plunging into a postseason funk.

Pettitte was gone that autumn, part of a three-year sojourn to his Houston hometown. Otherwise, Pettitte, Rivera, Jeter and Posada have been Yankees since 1995, through dynasty and drought and back to the top. They have each earned five championship rings, one more than Babe Ruth won for the Yankees, who will be honored with a parade in Manhattan on Friday.

It is the seventh championship for the principal owner George Steinbrenner, 79, who was not at Yankee Stadium on Wednesday.

Working on three days' rest, Pettitte, 37, looked ragged at times with five walks and three strikeouts. But he held up better than the Phillies' Pedro Martinez, 38, his old Boston adversary, who lasted just four innings.

Chad Durbin took over in the fifth, and Jeter, who finished 11 for 27 (.407), greeted him with a double. Mark Teixeira scored Jeter with a single, and after a walk, J. A. Happ came in.

Matsui ripped a double to deep right, scoring two runs to make it 7-1 and earning a share of a record. Only the Yankees' Bobby Richardson, in 1960, had driven in six runs in a World Series game.

The final out took 10 pitches, including four two-strike fouls from Victorino, a defending champion clinging to life.

A ground ball finally came, from Robinson Cano to Teixeira, who caught it and bolted across the diamond. Alex Rodriguez, the slugger who had never won before, greeted the throng with his arms in the air. Decorated champions embraced new ones, christening the ballpark the way they all expected. The championship was back to the Bronx, where the Yankees believe it belongs.

Tyler Kepner

Flanked by his longtime
pitching buddies, Mariano
Rivera and Andy Pettitte,
Jeter savors the victory
over the Phillies that
brings the Yankees their
27th world championship,
Nov. 4, 2009.
Photo: Barton Silverman,
The New York Times

"You forget how good it feels after the final out. But I appreciated the last ones we won. I knew it was very, very difficult to do. If it was easy, people would be repeating every year. No one's done it since we did."

DEREK JETER after the clubhouse celebration, *Nov. 6, 2009*

Ubiquitous Pinstripes and Chants to 'Go for 28'

Nov. 7, 2009 | The Yankees took one last ride together to celebrate their championship. It was a slow, joyous journey up Broadway, an outdoor party attended by hundreds of thousands of their closest friends. For the first time in nine years — and time is measured in dog years in Yankeeland — the Yankees and their fans could brag about being the best.

The cheering almost never quieted. Derek Jeter waved to so many people that he stopped feeling like a shortstop.

"You feel," Jeter said, "like you're the president, waving."

Joe Girardi admitted that the 2010 team would probably look a bit different from the club that vanquished the Philadelphia Phillies.

"I wish we could just continue to play," Alex Rodriguez said. "We have such a good group of guys. You know. No umpires, no scores. Just show up and have fun, like a softball game."

The Yankees' captain, accompanied by Minka Kelly, rides a float in the 2009 ticker-tape parade.
Photo: Kevin Kane, WireImage

Jack Curry

Flanked by Alex Rodriguez and Jeter, Robinson Cano (24) and Nick Swisher jump up to celebrate the Yankees' 6-1 victory over the Minnesota Twins at Yankee Stadium, completing a three-game sweep in the American League Division Series, *Oct. 9, 2010.*
Photo: Barton Silverman, The New York Times

Left to right, Kerry Wood, Mariano Rivera, Jeter and Andy Pettitte watch as their teammates go down in order in the ninth inning of Game 6 at Rangers Ballpark in Arlington. The Texas Rangers held the Yankees to three hits, won 6-1 and clinched the American League Championship Series, *Oct. 22, 2010.*
Photo: Barton Silverman, The New York Times

"They hit better than us, they pitched better than us, they played better than us."

DEREK JETER, who hit .231 in the championship series, on the Texas Rangers' domination of the Yankees, *Oct. 22, 2010*

Gillette is just one of a number of products that Derek Jeter endorses. *Photo: Jemal Countess, FilmMagic*

CHAPTER ⑤

OFF THE FIELD

Long before he signed contracts with the Yankees, Derek Jeter knew the responsibilities that came with such an agreement. From the start, baseball had never been a given for Jeter, who had to earn the right to play. His parents, Charles and Dorothy, demanded good grades and faithful adherence to a contract that outlined specific rules of behavior.

As a boy, Jeter's favorite player was Dave Winfield, the star Yankees outfielder who had his own charitable foundation. Jeter thought that would be a good idea, so as a rookie he started one, too, with an emphasis on steering children away from drugs. It was a natural fit, because of Charles Jeter's background as a therapist helping people with substance abuse problems.

Jeter was raised to believe in himself, show respect for others and know right from wrong. He has never lost those core values. By 1999, Jeter's fourth season, Michael Jordan had sought him out as a spokesman for his clothing brand, calling Jeter a role model who projects a positive image. It is one of many endorsements for Jeter, who has also appeared on "Seinfeld" and hosted "Saturday Night Live."

Yet Jeter has maintained some semblance of privacy, never talking about his dating life and carefully scripting public appearances. He squires starlets yet cultivates a certain air of mystery, like a certain Yankee icon from years ago.

Where have you gone, Joe DiMaggio? Perhaps his modern equivalent plays shortstop in the Bronx.

"When Derek does something like this, I'm as proud of him as when he does something in baseball."

DR. CHARLES JETER on his son's visit to the children's ward at Bronson Hospital in Kalamazoo, Mich., *Dec. 24, 1997*

Doing a Good Turn

Dec. 24, 1997 | There is a smoothness about Derek Jeter as he glides past the stuffed animals, the coloring books and the blocks to visit Kaitlin Hines in the children's ward at Bronson Hospital in Kalamazoo, Mich.

Kaitlin is playing in a miniature kitchen, so Jeter casually crouches beside the 18-month-old and asks her what is in the refrigerator. The little girl in Barney slippers does not realize she is hanging out with the shortstop of the Yankees, but she is happy that he is at her eye level. She hands him a plastic bagel. Jeter inspects it, tells Kaitlin it looks delicious and returns it to her. She quickly stuffs the bagel in her mouth, then grins.

The cute byplay causes everyone to smile. It is a welcome sliver of happiness in this fourth-floor setting because there is nothing pleasant about babies with intravenous needles in their bodies and 6-year-olds with leukemia.

"When Derek does something like this, I'm as proud of him as when he does something in baseball," said Dr. Charles Jeter, who coordinated his son's visit to his hometown two weeks ago. "This has a tremendous impact when Derek asks these kids how they're doing. It's important."

Jeter understands that. His parents prepared him to be more than a major league baseball player. They prepared him to be caring and thoughtful by stressing his responsibilities and by imploring him to be better than good. They even negotiated yearly contracts with their son, detailing what was expected from him. In academics. In athletics. At home. With friends.

"Derek had goals," recalled his mother, Dorothy, "but he knew if he wanted to play in the Little League all-star game or go to baseball camp, he better come home with a 4.0, he better have his behavior intact and he better make curfew or he wasn't going anywhere."

The strict approach obviously worked. The 23-year-old Jeter has thrived in his two years in treacherous New York, perhaps the toughest city for a young athlete, and has made the gossip pages only when there is speculation about his dating this supermodel or that pop star.

The disciplined upbringing also molded Jeter into someone who takes the time to sign autographs for children in wheelchairs and to offer encouragement that their families will remember for weeks. His visit to Kalamazoo was only the second time he had seen his family since the Yankee season ended in October and he is about to leave the country for 10 days, but these less fortunate families at the hospital still take priority.

Privately, Jeter conceded: "I hate hospitals. I don't do well in them." But he also said: "People look up to you if you play for the Yankees. I think you should do something to help out. Some players don't look at it that way. Off the field is when people look up to you even more. That's when your job starts. Baseball is the easy part."

Jeter surprised even his parents last December by starting the Turn 2 Foundation, a charitable organization designed to steer high-risk kids away from substance abuse. He asked his father to help. Charles Jeter, a 49-year-old therapist with a private practice treating patients with substance abuse or psychiatric problems, abandoned his position to immerse himself in the foundation.

Jeter had wanted to start a foundation since he was a child because Dave Winfield, his favorite player, had one. In its first year, Turn 2 has raised $305,000 and plans to expand to New York. Jeter's father barely blinked when he was asked if he had wanted to give up his job to share a dream with his son.

"I'm impacting more people this way than I was in private practice," said Charles Jeter, who is officially the foundation's executive director. "It wasn't a hard decision. I saw this as a chance to work with Derek beyond the father-son relationship."

Derek and Charles Jeter visit a children's hospital in Kalamazoo, Mich., shortly before Christmas 1997.
Photo: Blake J. Discher for The New York Times

Spend the day with the Jeters and it becomes obvious that the polite yet reserved Jeter of the Yankee clubhouse is much looser and funnier around his family. The father and the son seem more like brothers or best friends. After Jeter said it was too frigid to walk three blocks from the Turn 2 offices to the hospital, his father told him he was "getting soft."

Charles Jeter, who played shortstop at Fisk University, tried to motivate his son as a 10-year-old by showing him his scrapbook and by telling him he would get one if he became a good player. Asked how many pages were in the scrapbook, Jeter said, "About two," almost causing his father to gag on his soda.

Charles Jeter contended that his son was an eighth grader when he finally beat him in basketball. But Jeter said, "I think it was more like the fourth grade." When Jeter was asked if working together has made the two closer, he sighed and kiddingly said, "Yeah, we're too close now."

That's obviously not true. This is a family that cares deeply about one another and about others. "My parents are everything to me," Jeter said. "I've seen friends who don't have that relationship and I feel fortunate. I know how special it is."

Charles Jeter never knew that feeling as a child. He grew up in Montgomery, Ala., without a father. Dorothy Jeter, 45, who was born in Jersey City, said her husband's strong and soothing demeanor reminds her of her own father's.

"He listens and he's there," she said. "He's just a good dad."

Charles Jeter said: "What I experienced made me want to be there for my kids. It made me want to be a good father and be supportive. I wasn't lacking because I had a great mother, but it's important to have a male role model."

Jeter, who has an 18-year-old sister, Sharlee, is amazed that his father navigated through childhood without a father. "I couldn't imagine it because I have been spoiled," he said. "My parents have done everything for us."

And still do. Dorothy Jeter took off from her job as a credit manager to furnish her son's new home in Tampa, Fla., including the Christmas tree, because that is where the Jeters will celebrate the holiday. That is why Charles Jeter quit his job when his son wanted to create the foundation. That is why Jeter spent a rare day home at the hospital and at a meeting with 750 youngsters from western Michigan who had performed well in school. His father thought it would be good for Turn 2, so Jeter, the boss, obliged.

Jeter ended his visit to the hospital in the oncology wing, where a curious boy in a Dallas Cowboys T-shirt ambled toward him and his father. A hospital official asked an 11-year-old leukemia patient, Julio Martinez, to find the Yankee, and the boy incorrectly shook hands with the father of the Yankee. Then Julio asked in exasperated fashion, "Where's the rest of the team?"

But Jeter was not disarmed by the boy who did not know him. He teased Julio about his shirt and told him the Cowboys had had a horrible season. He autographed a baseball for the boy, gave him a high-five and, suddenly, Julio had a new hero.

Just as Jeter was about to depart, Julio whispered something to his mother and she nodded. The boy rushed to Jeter, hugged him and said, "Thank you for coming and Merry Christmas," creating another smile that radiated from an unlikely place. Make that two smiles.

Jack Curry

Infield Chatter

Sept. 12, 1999 | *Buster Olney of The Times moderated a conversation for the New York Times Magazine between two shortstops, Derek Jeter of the Yankees and Chris Fontenelli of Toms River East, a month after that New Jersey team, the 1998 Little League world champions, lost the game for the United States title in the 1999 Little League World Series tournament in Williamsport, Pa.*

Jeter: Before a big playoff game, I'm always anxious to get things under way.

Fontenelli: Yeah, I get a good night's sleep, and when I wake up, I have a good breakfast. Pancakes, all sorts of stuff. And before a game, one of my teammates, Eric, he always had a pack of Skittles he got from his dad. So he always gave me a handful, and every time he did, we won.

Jeter: For good luck, I rub Zim's head — Don Zimmer's head. He's been in the game for 50 years, so he basically knows as much as anyone.

Fontenelli: Last year, when the Toms River team won the Little League tournament in Williamsport, I was on the 11-year-old all-star team. Everyone was saying maybe they'd get back there next year, so it made me excited thinking that maybe I could go.

Jeter: I always wanted to play in Williamsport, but we were terrible when I was in Little League. So I never got the chance.

Fontenelli: Playing in front of all the fans, you're a little nervous at first. But after you get out there, you calm down.

Jeter: That was like me when I came to the Yankees. Obviously, the Yankees are filled with a lot of tradition. They're known to be winners. And before I knew it, we had won the World Series. Everything happened so quickly. Then we turned around and lost the next year. It was kind of a shock.

Fontenelli: In Williamsport, it was tough because everybody was out to get us. They were nice about it, though. I met one of the Japanese kids when we were practicing by the cage, and we shook hands and got our picture taken together. He was real nice, so I was kind of happy that they got to win. I told him, "Good game." That made me feel better about losing.

Jeter: When we lose or I have a bad game, I usually forget about it. Once a game's over with, you can't do anything to change it. My parents talk to me a lot. They joke around with me. My mom's usually the first one to tell me I had a bad game.

Fontenelli: My mom and dad will just say, "Shake it off." They know it's not that big a deal.

Jeter: You can learn a lot just by watching great players. When I was growing up, Dave Winfield was my favorite. In his prime, he was the best all-around athlete in all of sports.

Fontenelli: Derek Jeter is my favorite. When I went over to my first Yankees game, you were the only one out there signing autographs, and you signed my ball. You were my favorite before that, too, but that made up my mind.

Jeter: Thanks, Chris!

Jeter has been seen in public with such women as the singer Mariah Carey (below), the actress Jordana Brewster (top right) and Lara Dutta of India, Miss Universe 2000 (bottom right)— but he doesn't talk about them.
Photos: Stan Honda, Agence France-Presse/Getty Images (below); Barton Silverman, The New York Times (top right); Arnaldo Magnani, Liaison/Getty Images (bottom right)

Yankees' Jeter Has a Wonderful Life

Oct. 23, 1999 | When Derek Jeter eases out of the dugout at Yankee Stadium or glides along the streets of the Upper East Side or hustles through a hotel lobby in any city, it is fascinating to watch the people who find themselves near him. They point, they whisper, they nod. Some squeal.

"Regardless of whether you're in the spotlight, you have to be wary of how you're perceived," Jeter said on Thursday. "You don't want to get in trouble. If you are in the spotlight, you have to be more careful with what you do."

Jeter is the dynamic player who symbolizes these successful Yankees, the youngest player, the most popular player and maybe even the most indispensable player.

"To me," Joe Torre said, "he's the coolest cat in town."

Jeter is the most recognizable player on the best team in baseball, the lead actor in a prime-time show.

"He likes being that guy," Paul O'Neill said. "A lot of people don't need that and don't like it. He does."

The phone rings in Jeter's apartment or in a hotel room on the road every day with the same message from Charles or Dorothy, his parents, the same advice that they have given Derek since he was a boy in Kalamazoo, Mich.

Though he is one of baseball's premier players, has been on the cover of GQ and endorses everything from shoes to a cereal called Jeter's, their calls do not stop. If anything, they intensify.

"We tell him we hope he's making good decisions," Dr. Charles Jeter said. "He's been fortunate, so don't mess up. We tell him to be wary of who he's with. We do this often. We trust him, but we ask about everything. It's routine."

It is so routine that Jeter asked his parents, "Why don't you just use a tape recorder and leave it for me?"

Hank Aaron, the career home run king, sought out Jeter and introduced himself before the All-Star Game, causing Jeter to gush, "Can you believe that?" Jeter once stared up at a music video on a clubhouse television in Tampa, Fla., and expressed a desire to date the singer Mariah Carey, which he eventually did. Now he does not discuss Carey or other women he dates, figuring gossip writers can do their own reporting.

He is still a bachelor making $5 million in salary alone, meaning there are always temptations. Jeter says he is cautious, but still has fun, so those late nights he reportedly spends at the China Club, Moomba and Jimmy's Bronx Cafe cannot all be blamed on creative writers.

"Going out with Jeter," David Cone has said, "is like going with Elvis."

When Jeter was 16, he borrowed the family car and was supposed to sleep over at a friend's house. The teen-agers first visited a girl and tossed rocks at her window. Her father came out, and Derek and his friend ran, leaving the car unattended and running. The police came, Jeter's parents were summoned and Derek was grounded. Just nine years later, he answers questions about whether his life is perfect.

"It's not perfect yet," Jeter said. "It's getting there."

"I'm doing something that I've always wanted to do for as long as I could remember," Jeter said. "That's play shortstop for the Yankees, go to the World Series and win championships. It's like everything is this big dream story. If I was writing a story when I was younger, this is exactly how I would have written it."

Jack Curry

Unexpected Room Service

April 4, 2000 | There is a cheerleading convention at the hotel in Anaheim, Calif., where the Yankees are staying, and today, Derek Jeter poked his head out of his room to put down a room service tray — and was spotted by one of the cheerleaders. After that, a group of cheerleaders from Clifton, N.J., stood outside his door and did cheers for the Yankees.

Jeter was the host of "Saturday Night Live" — and a good-natured participant in several sketches, *Dec. 1, 2001.*
Photo: NBCU Photo Bank/Dana Edelson

His Sister's Winning Fight

May 13, 2001 | Derek Jeter sat beside Joe Torre in the dugout during Friday night's game, as he had done hundreds of times before, and told his manager that it was a good day. Then Jeter told Torre exactly why it was a good day. Jeter's sister, Sharlee, no longer had to worry about having Hodgkin's disease. Torre was shocked because he did not even know the 21-year-old woman had had cancer.

"It knocked me back a little," Torre said.

Jeter found out last November that his little sister, the feisty one, the one he had always considered the best shortstop in the family, had Hodgkin's disease. It was a month after Jeter had been named the most valuable player of the World Series and two months before he signed a 10-year, $189 million contract. Those baseball issues were secondary to his sister's undergoing chemotherapy treatments every two weeks for six months.

When the chemo finished on Thursday and doctors told Sharlee she would not need radiation treatments because there were no more signs of cancer, the Jeters were relieved. Other than telling a few friends, Jeter had kept his sister's condition private. The only reason he revealed the news was because "now it's a success story," he said.

"Our family is not immune to anything that goes on in society," Jeter said. "We never expect nothing like this to hit our family. It's just one of those things you have to deal with and, fortunately, it's over with."

Jeter is so close to Sharlee that they sometimes speak five times a day, and that was before she became ill. Sharlee gave a speech about Derek when Kalamazoo Central High School in Michigan honored him in 1996, thanking her brother for his honesty and support and calling him her hero. Jeter cried as she spoke and has the speech framed over his desk at home in Tampa, Fla.

Sharlee Jeter was an excellent high school softball player, and her dream was to attend Michigan and play in the Olympics, but she changed her plans, in part, because she was constantly compared to Derek. "He didn't have that shadow over him," she once said. "I had it every day of my life."

Sharlee continued a reduced class schedule at Spelman College in Atlanta while splitting her treatments between Atlanta and Manhattan.

Sharlee is disappointed that she will not graduate with her class this month and will have to wait until December to earn her bachelor's degree in mathematics, but Jeter told her to "look at the big picture." The big picture is that Sharlee strolled into Yankee Stadium on Friday night to watch her brother play for the Yankees and walked in cancer-free.

"She's 21 years old, man," Jeter said. "You don't expect this to happen at such a young age. But the good news is she doesn't have cancer anymore."

Jack Curry

Clouded Crystal Ball

Aug. 10, 2003 | When Derek Jeter was a rookie in 1996, a sporting goods company offered him $5,000 to sign 1,000 baseballs. The company backed out on the proposed deal because it wondered if the autographed balls would be a worthwhile investment.

Seven years later, that decision looks dubious. One memorabilia dealer said an autographed Jeter ball today runs about $250, which would have been a return of 4,900 percent.

Three-Ring Christmas?
Send in the Jeters

Dec. 23, 2003 | As a child, Derek Jeter's parents never took him to the circus, but he took them to one last Thursday night: the Big Apple Circus in Damrosch Park at Lincoln Center.

"I can't remember ever taking him to a circus," said his mother, Dorothy Jeter. "I think this was his first time."

Her boy certainly seemed to be catching on quickly. Sitting in a red wagon being pulled by a clown, Mr. Jeter beat a drum to some Christmas songs. Then he stopped and admitted, "I can't play drums whatsoever."

Mr. Jeter was promoting his Turn 2 Foundation, a children's charity. He sat next to Santa Claus and handed out toys to children who wore Jeter jerseys and Yankee caps.

What did little Derek used to ask for in Christmases past? Jeter family members, interrogated separately, had their stories straight.

His sister, Sharlee Jeter: "He used to love the Hulk. That was his favorite."

His father, Dr. Charles Jeter (flexing like a bodybuilder): "He always liked the Hulk doll. He would pose like this."

Derek Jeter: "I admit I was a huge Hulk fan. I was a fan of the Lou Ferrigno Hulk, from the TV series."

Corey Kilgannon, with Joe Brescia

A Sampling of Jeter's Endorsements and Products

(as mentioned in The Times over the years)

- Pepsi-Cola
- Wheaties
- Jordan Brand, Michael Jordan's line of sports apparel for Nike
- Skippy peanut butter
- FleetBoston Financial Corporation
- Gatorade
- Gillette
- Starting Lineup rookie doll
- Acclaim Entertainment baseball video game
- McFarlane Toys action figure
- Visa

Before the Yankees'
season-opening
two-game series in
Tokyo against the
Tampa Bay Devil Rays,
Jeter and Hideki Matsui
pose at the Tokyo
Dome, *March 27, 2004.*
Photo: Toru Yamanaka,
Agence France-Presse/
Getty Images

A Yankee Throws Out the Opening Accolade

Dec. 3, 2004 | Derek Jeter and Jesse Jackson were among those in the packed house that turned out for the gala opening of the Alvin Ailey American Dance Theater's season at City Center on Wednesday night. Mr. Jeter, star shortstop for the Yankees, even made a cameo appearance onstage as the evening's honorary co-chairman, with welcoming remarks.

Judith Jamison, the troupe's artistic director, introduced him and allowed that she wished she were 20 again. "Now that's an honorary chairman," she declared.

Mr. Jeter proved more than a pretty face: like other athletes invited in the past to read a prepared text about the Ailey company's virtues, he was literally a good sport. He ended by standing at ease, feet apart and hands behind his back, just before the company swung into "Love Stories," the premiere that was the heart of the evening.

Anna Kisselgoff

Athletes Practice the Giveback

Nov. 13, 2006 | According to its 2004 tax form, Derek Jeter's Turn 2 Foundation, which helps youths avoid addictions, raised $1.8 million that year, of which $250,000 came directly from Mr. Jeter. Turn 2 also holds down costs — unlike many athletes' foundations — because Mr. Jeter's parents and sister run the foundation and take no salary.

Giving, Not Receiving, Is His Signature

July 15, 2007 | Derek Jeter signed one baseball, then another and another. He leaned back in his chair in the visiting clubhouse at AT&T Park in San Francisco on Tuesday and exhaled. Soon, there would be more items for him to authenticate with his looping signature.

Every year, the All-Star Game is an autograph bonanza. Players sign dozens of baseballs, bats and jerseys. Many of the players act like fans and hustle for signatures, too. Not Jeter, the Yankees' shortstop. He left San Francisco with no autographs.

"I've always felt funny asking people to sign something for me," he said.

So, although the San Francisco Giants' Barry Bonds, who is about to become baseball's career home run king, asked Jeter to sign a jersey, Jeter requested nothing in return.

Jeter listed Bonds as the biggest star to ask for his John Hancock. But Yogi Berra, a Hall of Famer, and other former Yankees also line up at Jeter's locker like giddy fifth graders.

"I've had some of the players on Old-Timers' Day ask me to sign for them," Jeter said. "It's weird. I'll look at them and say, 'Are you sure you want me to sign this?'"

It is not shocking that Jeter avoids chasing autographs, since he prefers keeping things simple. To Jeter, pursuing autographs complicates things. Still, as Jeter gives his autograph without getting any back, he said, "I'll probably regret it when I get older."

Jack Curry

For Yanks and Hokies, a Game to Remember

March 19, 2008 | The buses wound through the Blue Ridge Mountains, taking the Yankees from the airport in Roanoke to the heart of a campus changed forever last April. Fans cheered from the sidewalks at Virginia Tech in Blacksburg, Va., snapping pictures and waving. If the players looked out the windows, they could see decals of memorial ribbons on the backs of many cars.

The buses stopped at Drill Field, the memorial site for the 32 victims of a gunman's rampage 11 months ago. The players and staff members, led by the Yankees' general partner, Hal Steinbrenner, walked solemnly in a semicircle, past the stone markers for the dead.

Derek Jeter was the first player off his bus. Near the far edge of the memorial was the stone for Michael Pohle, a biochemistry major from Flemington, N.J. On the ground beside it was a T-shirt with Jeter's name and number. A young woman named Marcy Crevonis stepped from the crowd.

"Derek, do you mind if I take a picture by my fiancé's stone?" she said. "I won't cry, I promise."

Jeter said he has felt like this before, after Sept. 11, when he wondered how baseball players could possibly help people recover from devastation. He still does not know, he said. Maybe they could simply make them smile.

Jeter told Crevonis she could have the picture if she smiled. She did.

"That's part of the reason that we're here," Jeter said.

As the principal owner George Steinbrenner watched coverage of the massacre last April, he was moved to help Virginia Tech. Steinbrenner donated $1 million to a memorial fund and asked team officials to arrange an exhibition game on campus.

Tyler Kepner

"It was weird the first time around, wearing a different uniform. I hadn't worn another uniform that represented anything other than the Yankees since high school. Even in the minor leagues, the different teams still represented the Yankees."

DEREK JETER on wearing not pinstripes but, with a "sense of pride," the red, white and blue uniform of the United States team again for the second World Baseball Classic, *March 2, 2009*

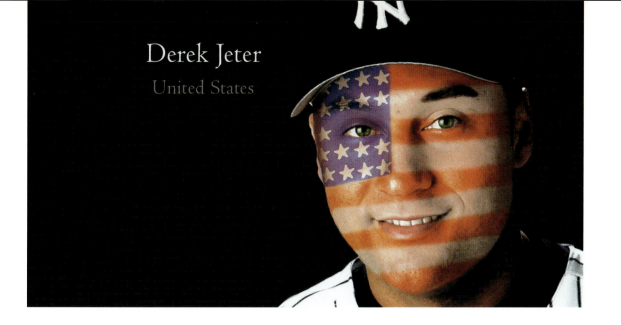

Derek Jeter
United States

Jeter Is Shortstop and Elder Statesman for U.S. Team

March 4, 2009 | Before Derek Jeter helped his temporary team defeat his regular team in an exhibition game on Tuesday in Tampa, Fla., he discussed his diplomatic duties as the captain of the United States team for the World Baseball Classic. Jeter's locker in the American team's clubhouse is between those of Jimmy Rollins and David Wright.

In that Rollins plays shortstop for the World Series champion Philadelphia Phillies and Wright is the third baseman for their bitter rivals, the Mets, Jeter joked about arbitrating between the two stars whose National League East teams sometimes trade trash talk.

"If they want to get at each other, they have to come through me," Jeter, the shortstop and captain of the Yankees, said, before his two hits and two runs batted in helped the American team to a 6-5 victory over the Yankees at Steinbrenner Field.

In that Jeter has four World Series rings and Wright none, Wright said he wanted to learn from a crosstown rival with New York savvy.

"As a young player in New York, you try to emulate certain guys," Wright said. "I'm excited to have a locker next to him and play next to him. Obviously, he's a class act. I'm interested to get in his head a little bit. This is a huge learning experience."

Joe Lapointe

"They don't strike out. Everybody puts the ball in play. They all run. The left-handers are halfway down the line when they put the ball in play. If I could do it or teach it, I would."

DEREK JETER on the Japanese players, after the United States team lost to Japan, 9-4, in the semifinals of the World Baseball Classic, *March 24, 2009*

Out of uniform, Jeter
showed up for an appear-
ance on the "Late Show
with David Letterman,"
Nov. 5, 2009 (above),
and went on location in
Brooklyn to play himself
as a homeless person
for a scene in the movie
"The Other Guys,"
Nov. 12, 2009 (left).
*Photos: Bobby Bank,
WireImage (above); Jeffrey
Ufberg, WireImage (left)*

Tribes of New York:
Derek Jeter fans in all shapes and sizes show their devotion with an assortment of attire — many jerseys showing his name, unlike the official Yankees uniform.
Photos: Fred R. Conrad,
The New York Times

"We've played together for 17 years, including the minor leagues coming up. You don't see that too often, especially with free agency. We're like brothers. To get an opportunity to spend all these years together and win another championship really feels good."

DEREK JETER on teammates Mariano Rivera, Andy Pettitte (back after three years with the Houston Astros) and Jorge Posada, following the 2009 World Series, *Nov. 6, 2009*

CHAPTER ❻

THE TEAM

Had Derek Jeter been drafted by the Houston Astros, the Montreal Expos or any of the other three teams that passed on him in the 1992 draft, his story would have unfolded so much differently. Looking back, it is hard even to imagine. Jeter and the Yankees seem to have been destined for a partnership, the player and the team bringing out the best in each other.

Playing for the Yankees put Jeter on a pedestal that has wobbled for others, exposing flaws and highlighting failures. Yet Jeter's character and performance have kept him sturdy all these years, and elevated the stature of a brand that had ebbed before he joined it.

So many giants of the game have come through the Yankees' universe in the Jeter years, and their relationships with Jeter have been scrutinized — none more so than Alex Rodriguez. The two had

been friendly rivals when Rodriguez played in Seattle, but his envy ultimately spilled over in public and changed the dynamics. When Rodriguez joined the Yankees in 2004, it was he, not Jeter, who moved from shortstop.

Other new arrivals have been smoother. Jeter welcomed Roger Clemens, a former foe, with good humor in 1999, and supported Jason Giambi after he was exposed for using steroids. Jovial teammates like Johnny Damon and Hideki Matsui helped foster a relatively harmonious clubhouse under Jeter's direction.

Of course, Jeter has not been alone in shaping the Yankees' modern culture of accountability, professionalism and winning. Andy Pettitte, Jorge Posada and Mariano Rivera also reached the majors in 1995, a bounty of young talent that helped restore the Yankees to glory.

Derek Jeter and Joe Torre —
the ideal player-manager
relationship — embrace
after the Yankees beat the
Boston Red Sox and clinch
a playoff spot, *Oct. 1, 2005.*
Photo: Vincent Laforet for
The New York Times

Jeter Is Still Torre's 'Little Boy' Shortstop

May 31, 1998 | In his third season as the Yankee shortstop, Derek Jeter is high among the American League leaders in batting, hits, runs, triples and stolen bases. On this Yankee juggernaut of a baseball team, he has been arguably its best player during what has been a dream season so far.

"And," the Yankee manager said with a smile, "he still calls me Mr. Torre."

Sitting in the Yankee dugout, Joe Torre was watching Jeter take batting practice.

"All that 'Mr. Torre' stuff doesn't bother me, but it bothers my wife," the 57-year-old manager was saying with a laugh. "She's a lot younger than I am, and he calls her Mrs. Torre."

"It's like Roy Campanella said: to play this game, you've got to have some little boy in you," Torre said. He was referring to the late Hall of Fame catcher for the Brooklyn Dodgers when Torre was growing up in Brooklyn. And now Torre's 6-foot-3-inch, 195-pound shortstop is playing baseball as if he were a little boy.

"Derek really seems to enjoy the game," Torre said. "I don't think many players do. The money. The celebrity status. The pressure. Not many players really enjoy the game anymore, but he does.

"You have to credit his parents. Derek's all business out there, but he knows when to have fun. I just hope he still enjoys it when he's making a lot of money and some people are saying he's not worth all that money."

Dave Anderson

From the beginning of the Joe Torre era in 1996 to the end in 2007, and beyond, Jeter has always had a special bond with the man he insists on calling "Mr. Torre" (or, sometimes, "Mr. T"). *Photo: Barton Silverman, The New York Times*

What Else Two Shortstops Talk About

March 30, 1997 | One of the highlights of the winter, said Alex Rodriguez of the Seattle Mariners, was the time he spent with Derek Jeter, the Yankees' Rookie of the Year shortstop. One of their frequent topics of conversation was something not directly related to baseball.

"That's the hardest thing for either of us to figure out — girls," Rodriguez said. "It's really hard. Trying to meet somebody you can trust. I don't know how you do it. I'm open for suggestions. That's not my area."

Yankees Give Clemens a Special Welcome

Feb. 27, 1999 | Buckingham Palace guards should take their work as seriously as Roger Clemens does. Even as he threw batting practice in Tampa, Fla., for the first time today, the Yankees' new pitcher focused deeply on the glove of catcher Jorge Posada, staring ahead. Clemens did not notice all the reporters circled round the batting cage, all the photographers, or what caused the coach Don Zimmer to bend over in laughter.

Clemens reached into a crate of baseballs, preparing to face the second batter of his session, and when he looked up, second baseman Chuck Knoblauch was standing at the plate, ready to hit, wearing a full set of catcher's gear. Mask, chest protector, shinguards, bat in hands.

Derek Jeter, standing next to the cage, wore the same suit of armor as Knoblauch; it was their own special way of honoring Clemens for the many times he had hit them with fastballs before he became a Yankee.

Clemens did a double take, before his face split into a grin that might have spanned Tampa Bay. Then he did what any self-respecting intimidator would do: he threw a fastball over Knoblauch's head, and did the same to Jeter.

All the participants thoroughly enjoyed this rite of passage.

"I knew something like that would happen eventually," said Clemens, aware of Jeter's promise that he and others would exact revenge on the hard-throwing pitcher. "For those two to step in with full gear like that did break the ice a little bit."

All is forgiven now that Clemens is with the Yankees. He will knock down opposing hitters in the months to come, no doubt, and his teammates will come to understand Clemens and understand why he does this. "You like him," Yankees Manager Joe Torre said, "once he's on your side."

Jeter took full credit for the idea of putting on the catcher's garb — "I thought of that one," he said, smiling broadly — and shared it with Knoblauch.

Buster Olney

Jeter congratulates Roger
Clemens on his 300th
win, *June 13, 2003*.
Photo: Vincent Laforet,
The New York Times

"There aren't too many teams in any sport where there is so much tradition and where so many players are showing up to remind you of it. When I first got here, I had a chance to play with Mattingly, and that was an honor. In spring training, you look up and you see Goose Gossage, and then walk around the corner and you see Reggie Jackson. You come here, and Yogi Berra is throwing out the first ball. You get spoiled around here."

DEREK JETER, *April 25, 1999*

An Agreement and a Division Among the Yankees

Aug. 14, 1999 | Eight days have passed since Chad Curtis criticized Derek Jeter for what he considered inappropriate behavior during a nasty brawl between the Yankees and the Seattle Mariners. After tense talks that night and another discussion that included an apology from Curtis two days later, the Yankees stressed that the disagreement was history. But, apparently, there is still a chill between the players.

Jeter has worked carefully to establish a pristine reputation with the Yankees. This was probably the first time that the best and most popular current Yankee had been criticized by a teammate, and it was definitely the first time it had occurred in such a public manner. So Jeter was asked if Curtis's criticism concerned him, and he chuckled before responding.

"Am I worried about it?" Jeter said. "No. I know exactly what you're saying. I mean, it's a situation where, hey, he didn't know what we were talking about. Unless you know what's going on, then you shouldn't approach someone in that manner."

Curtis noticed Jeter chatting amiably with Seattle's Alex Rodriguez, a close friend, and immediately confronted his teammate on the field and then again in front of reporters in the clubhouse.

Curtis felt that Jeter should not have acted in such a cavalier manner after Frankie Rodriguez just punched Joe Girardi in a skirmish at Safeco Field.

Jeter explained that Alex Rodriguez was talking with him about how Jason Grimsley had thrown an inside fastball near Edgar Martinez's head before hitting him, which helped precipitate the brawl. But Jeter told Alex Rodriguez that Jose Paniagua had basically done the same thing by throwing inside at Chuck Knoblauch and then drilling Jeter.

"We agreed to disagree on the issue, but I apologized in the manner I went about it," Curtis said. "You've got to take into context what was going on, the brawl and the adrenaline flowing and the way I approached him wasn't the way I should have went about it."

Jeter might be the premier player in the American League, so any condemnation of him, right or wrong, is noteworthy.

"He apologized," Jeter said. "But I didn't do anything wrong, so there's no reason to clear anything up."

Curtis clarified that by saying that he apologized for the execution of his actions, not the actions.

Jack Curry

Mr. October and Mr. November share some time behind the batting cage at Yankee Stadium, *Oct. 6, 2009.*
Photo: Richard Perry, The New York Times

Friendship of 2 Stars Is Safe After They Were on the Outs

Feb. 16, 2004 | Alex Rodriguez was a high school senior the first time he spoke with Derek Jeter. Rodriguez was expected to be the first choice by the Seattle Mariners in the 1993 amateur draft, but true to his already poised approach, he contacted a fellow shortstop, Jeter, about being picked in the first round by the Yankees a year earlier.

The fact-finding call led to more calls, more chats between two baseball-crazed teenagers, and the discussions stretched well beyond baseball.

Soon, two players with different backgrounds and similar goals developed a strong friendship that grew as they climbed toward the major leagues.

Jeter slept at Rodriguez's house when the Yankees were in Seattle, and Rodriguez would find a bunk in Jeter's apartment when the Mariners traveled to the Bronx. Rarely have two higher-profile opponents been as close.

"At this point," Rodriguez once said, "Derek has become like my brother."

But the friendship took a turn when Rodriguez said some unflattering things about Jeter three years ago in an article in Esquire. The implication was that Jeter was benefiting from being in a better situation with the mighty Yankees and that he was not as talented as Rodriguez.

Publicly, Jeter mostly ignored the static created by Rodriguez's remarks. But the words bothered Jeter, and so did having to answer questions about the depth of his friendship with Rodriguez.

After Rodriguez maligned him, Jeter retreated and their friendship cooled. Jeter, who could not be reached for comment yesterday, has said that he can make a quick decision to end a friendship if he feels wronged, which is what seemingly happened with Rodriguez for a spell.

The passage of time and Rodriguez's explanation of how a few critical comments should not undermine dozens of laudatory remarks he had made about Jeter over the years reduced the tension.

The soul brothers who separated and regained some footing in their friendship after a verbal slip-up will be in the highest of high-rent districts on the left side of the infield at Yankee Stadium. That will become a reality if Commissioner Bud Selig approves the trade today, as expected.

Rodriguez is considered the best player in baseball, and he was chasing the title of the best shortstop in major league history, but he was so desperate to leave the Texas Rangers that he surrendered his love affair with shortstop and agreed to move to third base.

Tall, regal and eloquent, Rodriguez seems to relish the spotlight and will instantly swipe a big part of it from other marquee Yankees.

For all of Jeter's appearances on the gossip pages, he works diligently to keep his private life private. When Jeter talked about his friendship with Rodriguez, he would usually describe it as close; it was Rodriguez who used terms like brothers.

Jeter and Rodriguez probably never discussed playing together. They both played shortstop, so there did not seem to be any way they would ever unite.

Rodriguez will be a Yankee soon, and now the question for Jeter is what it will be like to play alongside his old phone friend, not against him.

Jack Curry

"I'd like to take this time to put this all to rest right now. This move would not have happened unless Alex Rodriguez moved to third base. You go with the man who brought you to the dance, and you stick with him. Derek Jeter continues to get us to the dance. You don't mess with success."

GENERAL MANAGER BRIAN CASHMAN on widespread speculation that the newest Yankee, a two-time Gold Glove winner at shortstop, would push Derek Jeter to another position, *Feb. 17, 2004*

Mariano Rivera and Charles Jeter, Derek's father, enjoy one of many World Series celebrations, *Nov. 4, 2009.* Photo: Barton Silverman, The New York Times

Jeter and Rivera Share the Longest of Bonds

Oct. 14, 2004 | When Derek Jeter was a 19-year-old shortstop for Class A Tampa, Manager Jake Gibbs watched him play a few games before giving him the green light on the bases. Gibbs trusted Jeter's instincts so much that he was comfortable letting him decide if and when he should try and steal.

Ten and a half years later, Jeter is still that same kind of instinctive player for the Yankees, a player who seems to know what he is doing and when to do it.

Last night he walked, stole second base and scored the first run as the Yankees silenced the Boston Red Sox, 3-1, in Game 2 of the American League Championship Series. Mariano Rivera notched the last four outs for his second consecutive save. Jeter and Rivera, tethered for 11 years, were successful together again.

"Me and Mo, we've been together the longest of anybody here," Jeter said. "You appreciate someone as a player but more so as a player the more you get to know him."

Jeter, who is usually cautious with everything he says, is not careful in rating Rivera. "He's the best of all time," Jeter said.

While Jeter and Rivera did not become major contributors with the Yankees until 1996, they were minor league teammates in 1993, 1994 and 1995 and have a stronger baseball bond than any other Yankees.

"Jeter is a guy that I've been with for so many years," Rivera said. "We have that kind of relationship that I don't think nobody can break."

Their bodies have changed, but their minds and goals have not: have fun, win, then repeat the process.

Jack Curry

There's Jeter at Short, Yes, but Who's on Second?

May 10, 2005 | It is no big deal anymore, Derek Jeter says, barely an inconvenience. Change has become his routine, his expectation. It is the lifestyle he has become more wedded to than any double-play partner.

Miguel Cairo in the American League Championship Series last fall, Tony Womack in April, Robinson Cano in May and who can say come September? "At this point, you can pretty much throw anybody out there," Jeter said. Jeter shrugged with resignation, not indifference, and added, "It doesn't make any difference."

Second base is the bag of demarcation at Yankee Stadium, the place where legend merges with doubt, where Jeter's reputation as the archetypal winner blurs with the Yankees' dreadful start to 2005. A few steps to the left, embodied by Jeter, the future Hall of Fame shortstop, the four-championship dynasty is alive and well. To the right, uncertainty reigns in the presence of Cano, a rookie hitting .087.

"I really like this kid," said Luis Sojo, the third-base coach, infield instructor and fourth-ranked Yankee in career games started at second base with Jeter at short. "He's been struggling, but he doesn't look like it's affecting him. He's got a quick bat, so we know he's going to hit. For now, we just want him to make the plays."

Then Sojo dared put the most optimistic spin he could think of on a shaky situation. "I think he could be there for a long time," he said.

Jeter has heard that one before, when the Yankees acquired Chuck Knoblauch before the 1998 season and when Alfonso Soriano was swatting home runs all over the American League a few years later. "When we got Knoblauch, he was arguably the best second baseman in baseball, him and Roberto Alomar," Jeter said. "Then he had his throwing problems, and we had Soriano, and everyone said we were going to be the double-play combination for the next 10 years. Seemed like 10 weeks later, it was somebody else."

Soriano and Knoblauch lasted longer than that, enough to rank first and second in games played on the ever-growing list of Jeter's double-play partners. For now, Cano ranks 19th, last among the starters but gaining on Andy Fox, Wilson Delgado and Robert Eenhoorn. Remember Dave Silvestri? Of course you don't, but he is one of three others, including Jim Leyritz and Charlie Hayes, to sub a few innings, swelling the Jeter partner count to 22, according to Rick Cerrone, the Yankees' director for media relations.

That's an average of more than two second basemen a year, or more than the number of gloves Jeter has gone through in a decade. "One a year for the games and one for batting practice," he said, admitting it was easier to become more attached to his equipment because gloves don't get traded or moved to left field, like Womack, after one miserable month.

The first Yankee second baseman he played with? "Randy Velarde, when I came up in '95," he said.

The second baseman he has been most comfortable with? "That's tough, because I really haven't played with anyone that long."

The best athlete he has played with? "Soriano, easy."

His worst double-play partner?

"Leyritz, definitely."

Good, bad or somewhere in between, Sojo said he had never seen Jeter change his approach, his work ethic or his cooperative spirit. "The guy just wants to be on the field, just wants to play baseball," Sojo said. "He'll talk with you, work with you. If you can't play with this guy, then you can't play with anyone."

Harvey Araton

Luis Sojo, one of Jeter's longest-lasting double-play partners at second base and then one of his coaches, gets some help strething before a game, *Oct. 27, 1999*. *Photo: Barton Silverman, The New York Times*

Rodriguez Doesn't Sugarcoat Rift With Jeter

A rift? Close friends? Something in between? On the field, all that matters is that Jeter and Alex Rodriguez are teammates trying to help the Yankees win. *Photos: Gene J. Puskar, Associated Press (above); Steve Nesius, Reuters (opposite)*

Feb. 20, 2007 | For years, Alex Rodriguez has encouraged speculation by pretending he and Derek Jeter were still close. Earlier this month, he insisted they were great friends and said, "Things couldn't be better." On Monday in Tampa, Fla., Rodriguez tried a new approach: honesty.

"Let's make a contract," Rodriguez told reporters. "You don't ask about Derek anymore, and I promise I'll stop lying to you."

Rodriguez went on to admit that he and Jeter were not the buddies they once were, while stressing that they function well as teammates.

"We were best of friends about 10, 13 or 14 years ago, and we still get along well," Rodriguez said. "We have a good working relationship. I cheer very hard for him, and he cheers hard for me, and, more importantly, we're both trying to win a world championship. We'll leave it right there."

Asked why he decided to make that admission, Rodriguez said it was time to be truthful. Covering up the obvious, he said, made people suspicious.

"People are just assuming that things are a lot worse than what they are," Rodriguez said. "They're not. But obviously, it's not as good as it used to be, when we were blood brothers."

Catcher Jorge Posada, who is probably Jeter's best friend on the Yankees, said the relationship between Jeter and Rodriguez had no bearing on the field.

"Not everyone can be friends," Posada said. "They help each other out. That's all you can ask for. They seem to get along fine to me."

Tyler Kepner

Jeter Says There's No Rift, and Means It

Feb. 21, 2007 | A soap opera gave way to a baseball practice, and Derek Jeter and Alex Rodriguez were teammates. That relationship, they insist, is the only one that matters.

"On the field and in the clubhouse, our relationship is fine," Jeter said before the workout in Tampa, Fla. "Away from the field, people want to keep tabs on how many times we go out to eat. That has no bearing on what we're trying to do on the field."

Jeter strongly dislikes topics that deal with his life away from the ballpark. He also has little patience for reporters making assumptions. So it was not surprising that Jeter was irritated by the line of questioning he knew he would hear Tuesday.

"I don't have a rift with Alex," Jeter said. "We go out there, we work together. This is our fourth year together. It's annoying to hear about it all the time. Everyone assumes they know what our relationship is. They see us on the field. If one person gives another one a look, it's a story. If we're at opposite ends of the bench, people say it's a story."

Jeter and Rodriguez said they would not discuss the topic anymore. Jeter said he addressed it only because Rodriguez brought it up, and he was not as revealing.

"I understand my job is public," Jeter said. "But your private life is your private life. Once you open that door, it never stops. I don't feel it's necessary to talk about things that don't have to do with baseball. It doesn't have an impact on anything."

Tyler Kepner

Jeter Remembers Rizzuto as a Positive Influence

Aug. 15, 2007 | Derek Jeter does not collect autographs and is not sentimental by nature. But he has always maintained that a certain signed photograph in his home office carries special significance. It is a picture of Jeter with Phil Rizzuto, his forefather as a champion Yankees shortstop and his unabashed fan.

"You always remember the way people treat you, especially when you're coming up," Jeter said.

Before Jeter established himself as a star, Rizzuto treated him with reverence. When Jeter reached the majors in 1995, Rizzuto told the Yankees' manager, Buck Showalter, that he was making a mistake by not playing him more.

"From the time he stepped on the field, I watched him," Rizzuto said of Jeter in 2006. "He kept getting better and better."

Before first-pitch ceremonies or Old-Timers' Days, Rizzuto, who died Aug. 13 at 89, would seek out Jeter and offer encouragement more than advice. Jeter, a perennial optimist, connected with Rizzuto over their dispositions.

"He was just always positive," Jeter said. "It's always great when you have players that you respect and had played the game and been successful, and they go out of their way to tell you nice things. That's good to hear."

Yankees Manager Joe Torre said Rizzuto would show up at Yankee Stadium with his fellow Hall of Famer Yogi Berra, asking enthusiastically to see Jeter. Jeter's affection for Rizzuto, and his respect for his playing career, meant a lot.

"Whether it was the shortstop connection or spending their whole career in a Yankees uniform, there was an automatic bond there," Torre said.

Jeter is 6 feet 3 inches, 9 inches taller than Rizzuto, and he said he was amazed at how small Rizzuto was. Jeter would joke about it, and Rizzuto took the ribbing with good humor. Deep down, though, players knew that Rizzuto could not have been a pushover to succeed at 5-6.

For the rest of the season, the Yankees will wear Rizzuto's No. 10 in black on the left sleeves of their jerseys.

Tyler Kepner

'A Friend for Life'

Oct. 24, 2007 | Derek Jeter made his first public comments since Joe Torre rejected the Yankees' one-year contract offer last week. "He is a friend for life, and the relationship we have shared has helped shape me in ways that transcend the game of baseball," Jeter said in a statement released by the team. "His class, dignity, and the way he respected those around him — from ballplayers to batboys — are all qualities that are easy to admire, but difficult to duplicate. I have known Mr. Torre for a good majority of my adult life, and there has been no bigger influence on my professional development. It was a privilege to play for him on the field, and an honor to learn from him off the field."

Mutual admiration: Jeter and one of his biggest fans, Hall of Fame shortstop Phil Rizzuto, who threw out the ceremonial first pitch before Game 2 of the championship series against the Boston Red Sox, *Oct. 14, 1999.* *Photo: Mark Lennihan, Associated Press*

A Warm Welcome Helps
Pettitte Get Back to Work

Feb. 20, 2008 | On Andy Pettitte's first official day of spring training Tuesday, his teammates hugged him, the fans cheered him and reporters gradually changed the subject from his use of human growth hormone to his hopes for the 2008 season.

At his Monday news conference, Pettitte said he was cheered by the presence of the veterans Derek Jeter, Jorge Posada and Mariano Rivera. Pettitte said the support of his three teammates "made me want to cry."

Jeter said Tuesday that the veterans showed up because they have known Pettitte since all of them met in the minor leagues in the early 1990s.

"We're more than teammates, we're friends," Jeter said. "This is a guy you've played a long time with, spent a lot of time with, we have a lot of respect for. We're supportive. Whether people make mistakes or not, you still support them."

Joe Lapointe, with Alan Schwarz

Jeter Adjusts to a New Joe

Feb. 21, 2008 | Derek Jeter, the 33-year-old captain, first joked when comparing the new Joe with the old Joe. "He's got a little different walk," Jeter said of Girardi. But then Jeter turned serious when reflecting on what it would be like to play for a different manager after having only one for almost all of his 12-year career.

"So, yeah, today it sunk in, Mr. T's gone and Joe's here," Jeter said, using his nickname for Torre. "It's weird not seeing Mr. T. I've always said through the years I couldn't imagine playing without him. Now, I can."

Watching a fly ball during batting practice, Jeter and Alex Rodriguez flank their manager, Joe Girardi — whom Jeter calls Joe, not "Mr. G."
Photo: Chang W. Lee,
The New York Times

When Giambi Needed Him, Jeter Was There

Sept. 25, 2008 | Today, some of the beat crew wanted to talk with Jason Giambi as he finishes his seventh (and probably final) season with the Yankees.

Giambi said the years flew by, he's had the time of his life, and he's loved every minute. But that's really not true. He had no fun that winter day in 2004 when the San Francisco Chronicle published his testimony to the Balco grand jury acknowledging the use of steroids.

It was then, Giambi said, that he was glad to have Derek Jeter in his corner. "Jeet stepped up at a big time of my life, when I needed it," Giambi said.

What, precisely, made such an impact?

"He said, 'He's my teammate, he's my friend, and we'll welcome him back,'" Giambi said. "It was a very controversial issue for who he is and what he represents, and for him to do that, I'll never forget that. That's the type of guy Jeet is. He knew I was going through a tough time and he wanted to lend a hand out."

Tyler Kepner (online Bats blog)

Longtime teammates Mariano Rivera, Andy Pettitte, Jeter and Jorge Posada sit in front of other Yankees attending the press conference at which Alex Rodriguez admitted he previously used steroids, *Feb. 17, 2009. Photo: Al Messerschmidt, Getty Images*

"Everyone is disappointed, but you're there to support him and get him through it."

DEREK JETER on showing up for Alex Rodriguez's press conference, *Feb. 19, 2009*

Jeter Declares His Independence from the Steroids Era

Feb. 19, 2009 | Derek Jeter subtly expressed his support for Alex Rodriguez as Rodriguez grapples with repercussions from admitting to steroid use. But Jeter was much more forceful in distancing himself from any connection to the steroid era and, ostensibly, any connection to what Rodriguez did.

After the Yankees finished their first full-squad workout on Wednesday in Tampa, Fla., Jeter parked himself in the first-base dugout to discuss his teammate. He described Rodriguez's situation as the biggest distraction during his 14 seasons with the Yankees, but he was chiefly focused on separating himself from the cheats.

"One thing that's irritating and really upsets me a lot is when you hear people say that everybody did it," Jeter said. "Everybody wasn't doing it."

As the Yankees' captain, it is Jeter's responsibility to help Rodriguez through what will no doubt be a stressful season. The two have a complicated relationship, one that has dwindled from best buddies to co-workers. Jeter said he did not condone Rodriguez's behavior, but, as someone trying to snare another title, he has a vested interest in helping Rodriguez succeed.

"I think everybody is disappointed," Jeter said. "He's disappointed in himself. It's one of the things that he stressed yesterday. He's admitted it."

Although Jeter's scheduled interview was expected to center on Rodriguez, he massaged the message to emphasize his dissatisfaction with the perception of an era. Since so many players from the last 15 or so years have been tied to performance-enhancing drugs, Jeter offered a reminder that there were innocent players, too.

"The thing that I was most frustrated with is people making this blanket statement that it was the steroid era and everybody was doing it," Jeter said. "I've heard that on more than one occasion. That's not true. That's the thing that's most upsetting to me."

Over the years, Jeter has admitted that he has had discussions with teammates about who "might be doing this or might be doing that." After a player belted a mammoth homer, Jeter said he and teammates probably wondered aloud if the player was using performance-enhancing drugs. Jeter, whose father, Charles, was a drug and alcohol counselor when Jeter grew up in Kalamazoo, Mich., said no player had ever recommended that he try steroids.

"I understand people have questions," Jeter said. "I understand there are a lot of big names coming out. But that's not everybody."

If Jeter's repeated references to the notion that there were clean players in the steroid era did not make his point clearly enough, he provided one closing mention.

"I've never taken performance-enhancing drugs, I've never taken steroids," Jeter said. "I mean, that's it."

Jack Curry

Old Guard Fights On

Oct. 23, 2009 | The last game at the old Yankee Stadium was over, Derek Jeter had offered a spirited speech to the fans and players had scooped up some dirt as a memento. Still, there was something left to do. For four Yankees, it was time to acknowledge what they had done together.

So Jeter, Andy Pettitte, Mariano Rivera and Jorge Posada, who all made their debuts with the Yankees within five months of each other in 1995, gathered behind the mound. The players wrapped their arms around each other's shoulders and smiled for a picture, a picture that spoke of their sustained success.

Fourteen years and about 14,000 stories after those debuts, all four were at Angel Stadium of Anaheim for Game 5 of the American League Championship Series on Thursday.

"The relationships we have are important," Posada said. "It's camaraderie we've shared."

The picture of the four Yankees hangs in Posada's memorabilia room in his home in Florida. As important as it is to Posada, there is some disappointment linked to it because it was snapped in a year when the Yankees failed to make the postseason.

Pettitte was the first of the quartet to make his debut, which occurred on April 29, 1995. Rivera followed Pettitte to the Yankees 24 days later. Jeter joined the party six days after Rivera and stayed briefly. Posada was summoned in September.

The four players made drastically different contributions as the Yankees grabbed the wild card that season. Pettitte won 12 games and was a surprisingly steady left-handed starter. Rivera started more games than he relieved and notched five victories. Jeter played 15 games at shortstop. Posada barely has the season on his baseball card as he played in only one game.

While Jeter, Posada, Rivera and the Yankees have not been to the World Series since they lost to the Florida Marlins in 2003, Pettitte was actually there more recently. Pettitte, who signed a free-agent deal with the Houston Astros before the 2004 season, lost to the White Sox in the 2005 World Series.

In 1995, Pettitte was unsure if he should buy furniture for his place in New York because he did not know if he would last the season. Jeter ate at McDonald's on his first road trip. Rivera wanted to be a starter, not a reliever. Posada scored one more run in the postseason than he did in the regular season, when he never reached base.

The Yankees lost to the Seattle Mariners in torturous fashion in the 1995 division series. One year later, the trips to the World Series began. With one more win, the Franchise Four will make that rewarding journey again.

Jack Curry

Jorge Posada, Mariano
Rivera, Derek Jeter and
Andy Pettitte create one
more memento of their
years together at the
original Yankee Stadium,
Sept. 21, 2008.
Photo: Al Bello, Getty Images

◄ During the pregame presentations of world championship rings, Yankees embrace former teammate Hideki Matsui in his first return to the Bronx, *April 12, 2010*. *Photo: Jim McIsaac, Getty Images*

► Jeter greets the rest of his team — both live, bottom of photo, and on Yankee Stadium's giant Diamond Vision screen, top — after receiving his World Series ring. *Photo: Barton Silverman, The New York Times*

Getting Rings, Then Getting to Work

April 10, 2010 | The final game at Yankee Stadium last season ended with Mariano Rivera saving a victory for Andy Pettitte. The Yankees returned on Tuesday to collect their championship rings, and three hours later Rivera secured another win for Pettitte. The Yankees are trying to move past their accomplishments from 2009, but days like this recall the glory they hope to sustain.

Behind six shutout innings from Pettitte and home runs by Derek Jeter and Nick Johnson, the Yankees raced to a big lead against the Los Angeles Angels. They continued their seamless transition between Game 6 of the World Series and Game 7 of the regular season by turning to Rivera to finish off a 7-5 victory. Among them, Pettitte, Rivera and Jeter have 15 rings. The other player with five, Jorge Posada, added three hits and drove in a run.

"Everyone talks about how long we've been here," Jeter said. "In our minds, it's like we're just little kids. We just want to come out here and contribute and be consistent."

On a day the Yankees celebrated their past, Rivera silenced Hideki Matsui, the most valuable player of last year's World Series, to clinch their third straight win.

In his return to the Bronx, Matsui received the longest and loudest reception during the pregame ring ceremony, but for the first time in eight years, Yankees fans did not mind that he went 0 for 5. By the end of the first inning, the crowd of 49,293, the largest to see a regular season game at the new ballpark, was cheering for Johnson, Matsui's replacement at designated hitter, who homered deep into the seats in right-center field.

For many players, watching Matsui receive his ring was the second best part of their day. Gene Monahan, the beloved longtime trainer who missed spring training because of an undisclosed illness, surpassed that. During the ceremony, Monahan was called forward first, and the Yankees honored him by having him stand alone with his ring by first base.

The very first ring, though, was presented about 20 minutes before the ceremony began, when Jeter and Joe Girardi visited the suite of the principal owner, George Steinbrenner. There, Steinbrenner took off his 2000 World Series ring to make room on his finger for the new one, crafted from white gold and featuring a blue stone beneath a diamond-embossed Yankees logo. "Quite frankly," said his son Hal, the managing general partner, "I think he was almost speechless."

Ben Shpigel

Jeter Follows Only One Voice

July 12, 2010 | Players have long tried to imitate the rich, authoritative tones of Bob Sheppard, the Yankees' beloved public-address announcer, who died Sunday morning at 99. But, in the words of Mariano Rivera, his voice is "irreplaceable."

A moment of silence was held before the Yankees' game against the Mariners at Safeco Field in Seattle.

"You think of all the tradition with the Yankees, you think about Gehrig and Yogi and Joe D and Mantle, and I think you mention Bob Sheppard," Manager Joe Girardi said. "That's how important he was to this franchise. The first time I heard him was in 1996, the first time I walked out in Yankee Stadium, and you realize that you hit the big lights when Bob Sheppard announces your name."

It remains that way for Derek Jeter, who requested Sheppard record his voice to play before his at-bats. Jeter grew up a Yankees fan and said he would continue the tradition to honor Sheppard.

"He's the voice I always heard," Jeter said. "There were a few times sprinkled in and out when he wasn't there, and it just didn't sound right. So I got the idea to record his voice and to always use it."

Sheppard announced his final game Sept. 5, 2007, never visiting the new Yankee Stadium. But his voice will live on, in Jeter's at-bats.

Ben Shpigel

▶ Yankees owner George Steinbrenner signs autographs at Yankee Stadium on Aug. 11, 1994, the day of the last major league games of the season before a strike by players began, leading to the first cancellation of the World Series since 1904.
Photo: Librado Romero, The New York Times

◀ Bob Sheppard's voice is forever the one that will announce Jeter's at-bats, for as long as he's a Yankee.
Photo: Richard Perry, The New York Times

George Steinbrenner, 1930-2010

July 13, 2010 | The Yankees had more All-Stars on Tuesday in Anaheim, Calif., than any other major league team. They are the reigning World Series champions, with the best record in baseball. They have a gleaming new stadium in the Bronx and a thriving cable television network. Their empire is fully restored, the way George Steinbrenner wanted.

Steinbrenner, 80, left the stage Tuesday, just as baseball prepared for its annual summer showcase. The principal owner of the Yankees since 1973, he was the second grand figure of the franchise to die in three days. Bob Sheppard, the public-address announcer at Yankee Stadium from 1951 to 2007, died on Sunday at age 99.

Inevitably, their deaths will set a somber tone at Yankee Stadium for Saturday's Old-Timers' Day, one of many traditions of which Steinbrenner was proud caretaker. As demanding and meddlesome as he was in his heyday, nobody questioned Steinbrenner's reverence for the Yankees, who wore black armbands on Tuesday and will wear memorial patches the rest of the season.

"It's tough, because he's more than just an owner to me," said Derek Jeter, whom Steinbrenner named the team's captain in 2003. "He's a friend of mine. He will be deeply missed."

Jeter awoke Tuesday to a flurry of messages about Steinbrenner, and he said he was shocked. Jeter was planning to visit Steinbrenner in Tampa, Fla., sometime in the next two days. Jeter last saw Steinbrenner at the home opener in April, presenting him with his championship ring in the owner's suite at Yankee Stadium.

"I got a chance to tease him because he had an Ohio State ring and I told him to take it off now, and replace it with the Yankee ring," Jeter said. "Those are the memories that you remember, the intimate moments."

Jeter first met Steinbrenner in 1992, when he was 18 and had just signed as the team's first-round draft pick. From the start, Steinbrenner made clear his expectations: "We expect big things from you," he said.

No Yankee better reflected Steinbrenner's mission than Jeter, who shared the notion that no season could be successful without a World Series title.

Early in his career, Jeter said, he was doubled off third base on a line drive. After the game, Steinbrenner yelled at him for the mistake. It did not matter that the Yankees had won. Steinbrenner had no tolerance for failure.

"That rubbed off," Jeter said. "Whether it was the players, the front office, the people working at the Stadium, it didn't make a difference. He expected perfection."

Perfection is impossible, but Steinbrenner restored the culture in which the Yankees relentlessly pursue it. On the day he died, they were about as close as they could get.

Tyler Kepner

During a 20-minute pregame tribute to Bob Sheppard and George Steinbrenner, July 16, 2010, Jeter — the only Yankee to address the fans — called the two men "shining stars in the Yankees universe." Mariano Rivera placed two roses on home plate. Sheppard's recorded voice welcomed fans to Yankee Stadium one last time, but the public-address system was silent throughout the game. Clips of Steinbrenner were shown between innings. And the ardent fans known as the bleacher creatures skipped their first-inning roll call of the Yankees' lineup for only the second time since they began the tradition in 1996.

Photo: Uli Seit for The New York Times

Derek Jeter takes his rightful place next to the manager, Joe Torre, and coaches Don Zimmer and Mel Stottlemyre, *Oct. 5, 2002.*
Photo: Barton Silverman, The New York Times

> "He always has been the leader of this team; he's always been the guy that we look to. He's our captain. If there's anybody who's going to be the captain of this team, it's Derek Jeter."

JORGE POSADA, after George Steinbrenner called into question Derek Jeter's readiness to become the next Yankees captain, *Feb. 17, 2003*

CHAPTER **7**

CHARACTER OF A LEADER

The Yankees officially named Derek Jeter captain on June 3, 2003, at a hastily arranged news conference on a road trip to Cincinnati, of all places. It was one of the last truly impulsive acts of the principal owner, George Steinbrenner, whose influence would soon begin to wane. But the Yankees were slumping at the time, and Steinbrenner felt the urge to formally recognize what everyone had known for years.

Leadership came naturally to Jeter, who commands respect with his effort, his focus and his treatment of others in uniform. Just as he dismisses concerns about his age as a veteran, he never made an issue of it as a young player. Teammates did not question Jeter's example when he was in his early 20s. They simply recognized it, followed — and won, a lot.

In early 2001, after four championships in five seasons, Steinbrenner agreed to pay Jeter $189 million for 10 years. Less than two years later, he tested Jeter's resolve by questioning his commitment, citing Jeter's active social life. It was a laughable remark to those who knew Jeter, who was deeply influenced by his grandfather, Sonny Connors, a school and church handyman in New Jersey.

"He never missed work, if he was sick or he had a bad day," Jeter said after Connors died, on New Year's Day 1999. "He always seemed to go and work every day. I think that's something I learned from him."

Jeter has lived that virtue, and the Yankees have followed him to dazzling heights.

> # "Mrs. Jeter, he could've started here when he was in the eighth grade."
>
> **ACE ADAMS,** the former assistant baseball coach at the University of Michigan, responding to Dorothy Jeter's question about whether her son played well enough to make the team

Derek Jeter:
The Pride of Kalamazoo

April 9, 1999 | Ask around Kalamazoo, Mich., and everybody seems to have only good things to say about Derek Jeter and his family. Derek was the type of kid, Evelyn Lal said, "that you wanted your kid to be friends with."

Shanti Lal, her son, befriended Derek in the fourth grade, in Mrs. Garzelloni's class at St. Augustine Cathedral School in Kalamazoo. "Derek was one of those kids you just never forget, and I would say that even if he wasn't playing baseball," said Shirley Garzelloni, who retired last year. "He was the kind of student any teacher would want to have. I was just struck with how much he cared about his fellow classmates."

He appeared a little shy and quiet, she thought, but had a composed confidence, even as a boy. He got along with everybody and succeeded without needing to be prodded or praised. "He was completely self-motivated, creative, never wasted any time," Garzelloni recalled. "There are kids who will say to you, 'I don't have anything to do' — not with Derek. He always found something to do. I remember doing a report card and thinking, 'Does he realize just how intelligent he is?'"

He was comfortable around different types of people and, his father suggested, that made sense. Charles Jeter is black and from Alabama and Dorothy Jeter is white and from New Jersey, and Derek seemed at ease with kids from all kinds of backgrounds.

There were the trials of youth: Charles Jeter remembered that once when Derek was perhaps 10 or 11, a teacher told them that Derek had said something cruel to a classmate. His parents chastised Derek, told him this was unacceptable. You treat people the way you want to be treated, they said, and Derek thought about this quietly, absorbing and learning.

"He was pretty much head and shoulders above his contemporaries, but he never came across as being arrogant," said Chris Oosterbaan — Jeter stills calls her "Mrs. O" — who taught writing and history to Jeter at St. Augustine when he was in the seventh and eighth grade. "He didn't paint a glowing picture of himself, and he didn't have this 'I'm really cool' attitude. He was very genuine and humble."

Jeter worked as a tutor in a computer laboratory in his last two years of high school at Kalamazoo Central, and Sally Padley, who taught Jeter in British literature, thought he conducted himself perfectly. "He just had an easy manner, no signs of conceit, and when he was helping people, he didn't make any of them feel less important," Padley said.

She taught him in the last hour of school, a time when some

student-athletes departed to prepare for games. "He absolutely never asked for any special consideration," Padley recalled. "He never asked out of class, never bragged about his baseball."

But baseball was significant to him. His favorite team, Derek told his fourth-grade teacher, was the New York Yankees, and he wrote an essay in the eighth grade of his desire to play shortstop for the Yankees. Padley asked her 11th-grade students to create a coat of arms, unique to each of them and their personalities. In the center of Jeter's rendering, he included a picture of a Yankee at bat.

Dorothy and Charles Jeter were always involved, Derek's former teachers say, always at the teacher-parent conferences, supportive of their suggestions, interested in their input. "They have extremely strong values," Padley said. "They are some of the best parents I've ever seen."

When Derek said he wanted to be the shortstop for the Yankees, they told him that with hard work, anything was possible, and sometimes the four of them would go in their backyard to practice — Charles hitting ground balls, Derek fielding and throwing the ball to his younger sister, Sharlee, perhaps Dorothy pitching Wiffleball.

Ace Adams, formerly the assistant baseball coach at the University of Michigan, said the Jeters were the best parents of any recruit he ever dealt with. Adams recalled how, after the Yankees drafted Derek, the teen-ager informed him daily of the progress of his contract negotiations, so that the Wolverines would be prepared to replace Jeter if he signed.

It was apparent to Adams that Derek Jeter was going to be a star, yet he and his parents never took Adams or the school for granted. Dorothy Jeter once asked Adams, "Are you sure Derek is good enough to play here?" Adams replied, "Mrs. Jeter, he could've started here when he was in the eighth grade."

Padley, Oosterbaan and Garzelloni all spoke of their belief that no matter how big a celebrity Jeter became, no matter how much money he made, he would be rooted. "Derek has a lot of things he's going to learn about people, and being in the eye of the public," Padley said. "But I believe he's going to remain a very decent human being."

He's still Derek from Kalamazoo, with the same friends from high school, friends who are scattered around the country now. Doug Biro, a friend from the fourth grade, stopped by the other day to have dinner with him in Tampa, Fla.

Shanti Lal, his friend from Mrs. Garzelloni's class, visited him in the minor leagues in Columbus, Ohio, and in spring training two years ago. They grew up together, laughed together; Derek and Shanti and another friend had entered a talent contest, the three of them, as the Jackson Five, with wigs and blue suits.

Lal planned to go to medical school, but on May 4, 1997, his sport utility vehicle rolled over on Interstate 94, and he was thrown from it and killed. In the midst of a baseball season, Jeter could not attend his friend's service, but he wrote a letter, and his sister read the words aloud, about his friendship with Shanti, their shared experiences, their last days in Tampa together.

"Derek, he's a very good kid," Evelyn Lal said last week.

Buster Olney

For Jeter, Being Part of Yanks' History Is Priceless

Feb. 10, 2001 | When it became apparent several days ago that Derek Jeter's 10-year, $189 million deal was going to become official, he talked by phone with the Yankees' principal owner, George Steinbrenner. Not many players get this type of contract, Steinbrenner said, and Jeter understood the subtle message in the owner's words: we believe in you, and we expect you to lead.

"It's always been my dream to play for the Yankees," Jeter said yesterday, "and now I know this dream can last."

Jeter's contract — the result of many months of negotiating between the player's agent, Casey Close, and the Yankees' president, Randy Levine, and general manager, Brian Cashman — will produce the second-largest total payout in professional sports; only the $252 million contract signed by shortstop Alex Rodriguez with the Texas Rangers in December is larger. "It's a huge contract, it's a huge commitment," Jeter said.

Jeter was willing to forgo his right to become a free agent next fall and perhaps make more than $200 million. What he gets in return, beyond the money, is the peace of mind that he will most likely finish his career with the Yankees.

"Obviously, it's a lot of money," he said. "But it's not something where it really has set in; it's more of a feeling that I'm real happy to know I'm going to be with this organization. I'm really happy to know I'm not going to be going anywhere else."

So is Steinbrenner. "Derek Jeter embodies everything the Yankees are about," he said in a statement released by the team. "There are some things that can not be defined by batting average, home runs and runs batted in. They're important, but they cannot totally define a player's worth to a team. And you'd be making a mistake if you think they do. Equally important are an athlete's heart and desire. Derek exemplifies those qualities as well as any player."

Jeter's intangible contribution has been his injection of confidence and enthusiasm. He could lighten the mood of any mournful pitching change by slapping Manager Joe Torre on the chest with his glove and making a joke, and he has demonstrated, beyond any doubt, that he thrives in the spotlight. Last year, he became the only player to win the All-Star Game Most Valuable Player award and the World Series M.V.P. award in the same season.

Buster Olney

The Insatiable Desire to Win

Oct. 3, 2002 | Dr. Charles Jeter is unsure if his son was born with the insatiable desire to win, although he might have helped foster Derek's passionate approach by never letting him win in checkers.

"Psychologically, when people are telling you there are high expectations for you, I believe you can respond to that," Charles Jeter said. "When you set the bar high, you'll go for that. If you don't set it high enough, maybe you'll wind up settling."

As much as fans think that Jeter's success in the spotlight began with his first postseason game in 1996, he traces it back a dozen years to a basketball court in Kalamazoo, Mich. There were 3 seconds left and Jeter's Kalamazoo Central team trailed Portage Central by 2 points. Don Jackson, Kalamazoo's coach, designed a play in which Jeter, a skinny-as-a-fungo-bat sophomore guard, would attempt a 3-pointer.

Jeter broke free, dribbled once and drilled the winning jumper. The memory is 12 years old, but it still caused Jeter to giggle like a 15-year-old. "After that game, no matter what I was playing," Jeter said, "I always wanted to be out there with the game on the line."

Jack Curry

◀ The captain of the Yankees acknowledges the adulation of the crowd during his third ticker-tape parade following a World Series triumph, *Oct. 29, 1999.*
Photo: Chang W. Lee, The New York Times

▶ Jeter, who's never satisfied unless the Yankees win, shows his frustration after arguing in vain that he was safe at second on a close play in Game 2 of the American League Division Series against the Oakland Athletics, *Oct. 11, 2001.*
Photo: Barton Silverman, The New York Times

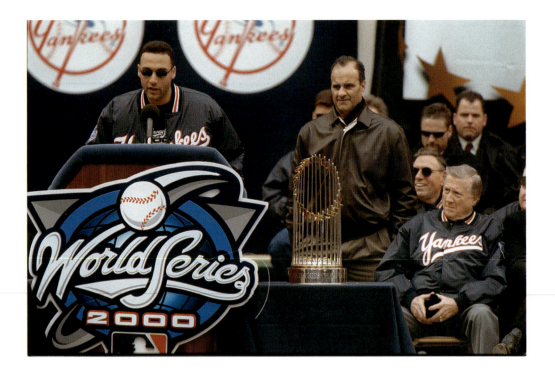

As Joe Torre and George Steinbrenner look on, Jeter speaks for the team at City Hall after the ticker-tape parade up Broadway, *Oct. 30, 2000.*
Photo: Marilynn K. Yee, The New York Times

With a leap onto home plate to end Game 4 of the 2001 World Series just after midnight on Oct. 31, No. 2 — but number one to his teammates and fans — acquires his new nickname: "Mr. November."
Photo: Chang W. Lee, The New York Times

"We've never given up until the last out. We always feel we can win. It doesn't happen all the time, but we believe it. That's the confidence we have."

DEREK JETER on the winning attitude he always has and always tries to impart to his teammates, *Nov. 1, 2001*

"There are a lot of people trying to push him to the appointment. I know Joe [Torre] would like to see it. Do we need a captain for this team right now? I'm not sure. His charities are tremendous. The other activities? I was young once. I know how it gets. But that's all I was trying to tell Jeter: concentrate and focus for me next year. He knows; I tell him right to his face."

GEORGE STEINBRENNER on his resistance to naming Derek Jeter the Yankees' captain, *Jan. 8, 2003*

Steinbrenner, Jeter and a Soap Opera

Feb. 23, 2003 | Two years ago, Derek Jeter took a 10-year, $189 million contract that he earned as the Yankees' indispensable and classy shortstop, but now he has to tolerate George Steinbrenner's wrath in a Yankee soap opera that won't disappear.

Jeter has to take it just as Reggie Jackson, Dave Winfield, Don Mattingly, Billy Martin, Yogi Berra and so many other Yankee players and managers had to take it during the principal owner's noisiest years.

Steinbrenner is a corporate chameleon. With strangers, he can be charming and charitable, especially if he wants something they've got. But if you're on his payroll, he feels entitled to do or say anything in order to get more production out of you — whether you're the Yankee Stadium receptionist or you're the Yankees' best player.

When the Yankees were winning four World Series championships in five years, the principal owner's relative silence had some people thinking he had mellowed.

Those people didn't understand. With all those new World Series rings and profits, Steinbrenner didn't have much to growl about. But ever since the Yankees were rudely eliminated in the first round of last year's American League playoffs by the Anaheim Angels, his bark has been as threatening as his bite.

"He's worse than ever," Yankee front-office people were heard to mumble in recent months. "Worse than the losing years."

Steinbrenner has always believed in the psychology of creative tension. Put a player on the spot. Put anybody in the organization on the spot, for that matter, but particularly a player. Particularly the best player, the highest-paid player.

When asked in a December interview with The Daily News if Jeter was a candidate to be the Yankees' first captain since Mattingly, the principal owner ignored the question.

"He wasn't totally focused last year," Steinbrenner said. "How much better would he be if he didn't have all his other activities . . . he makes enough money that he doesn't need a lot of the commercials . . . when I read in the papers that he's out until 3 a.m. in New York City going to a birthday party, I won't lie. That was a violation of Joe's curfew."

Jeter considered that to be a cheap shot at both the integrity of his bachelor lifestyle and his responsibility as a role model.

Although quietly angry, Jeter has calmly defended himself while wisely careful "not to say anything bad about Mr. Steinbrenner" to reporters at the Yankees' complex in Tampa, Fla. But the principal owner couldn't resist prolonging the situation. Asked if he thought his message had been received by Jeter, he snapped, "It better have."

When Steinbrenner later acknowledged that Jeter "always gives 100 percent, but I need 110 percent; let's put it that way," it confused Joe Torre.

"I sort of shake my head when I hear people say 150 percent or 110 percent," the manager commented. "I'm not sure there is more than 100 percent."

Jeter should ask Steinbrenner to read his autobiography that was aimed at teenagers, "The Life You Imagine: Life Lessons for Achieving Your Dreams" (Crown, 2000), written with Jack Curry, a sports reporter for The New York Times. In it, Jeter openly discussed his night life.

"I never drank or smoked in high school because it scared the heck out of me," Jeter wrote. "And even today, long before I ever walk into a club, I've thought about how I'd like my night to unravel and it always ends with me leaving sober."

Some professional athletes ignore the responsibility of a role model, but Jeter understands it.

"I believe in being a role model," he wrote. "I think anyone who says they're not a role model doesn't get it. If you play pro sports, you're automatically a role model. You can talk for hours about how kids should view their parents as role models and that's true. But when you're in the public eye and you're on TV, you're going to be a role model. You're going to have kids looking up to you and trying to emulate you."

In the book, Jeter recalled spurning offers of cocaine and pills from strangers in nightclubs.

"I can't say I won't make any mistakes because everyone does," he wrote. "But I can unequivocally tell you that my morals and values won't change in the next week or the next 20 years. That's something I control and something I know won't change."

The problem is George Steinbrenner won't change either.

Dave Anderson

"He's the boss and he's entitled to his opinion, right or wrong, but what he said has been turned into me being this big party animal. I don't think that's fair. I have no problems with people criticizing how I play. But it bothers me when people question my work ethic. That's when you're talking about my integrity."

DEREK JETER on media coverage of George Steinbrenner's criticism, *Feb. 14, 2003*

Echo of '78:
Steinbrenner in an Ad

May 30, 2003 | In 1978, George Steinbrenner and Billy Martin starred in a commercial selling Miller Lite in which they engaged in the campaign's long-running "tastes great/less filling" debate. In that summer of Yankee discord and malcontents, Steinbrenner "fired" Martin in the commercial. "Oh, not again!" Martin replied.

Steinbrenner is back, satirizing another feud, this one his spat with Derek Jeter over what he said were the shortstop's late hours and lack of focus last year. This time Steinbrenner wanted to challenge Jeter, not fire him. But like Martin before him, Jeter plays the foil, one with far more job security than Martin ever had.

Their Visa commercial, which starts next week, opens with Steinbrenner, in blue blazer and white turtleneck, ushering Jeter into his office.

"How can you possibly afford to spend two nights dancing, two nights eating out and three nights just carousing with your friends?" he asks. Jeter, who never says a word, flashes his Visa card (Steinbrenner is mightily impressed) and the action cuts to a flashy club where Jeter is the leader and Steinbrenner plays the caboose of a conga line.

Richard Sandomir

Steinbrenner Appoints Jeter Captain of the Yankees

June 4, 2003 | Derek Jeter has been an established Yankees star for years, and the highest-paid player on George Steinbrenner's team since February 2001. But Steinbrenner, the principal owner, waited until today to make official what the players in the clubhouse already knew: that Jeter is the captain of the Yankees.

Steinbrenner did not show up for the announcement at Great American Ball Park in Cincinnati before the Yankees lost to the Cincinnati Reds, 4-3, choosing instead to stay in Tampa, Fla., to oversee today's amateur draft. But it was Steinbrenner's decision alone, and he appointed Jeter at this moment — on the road, with the team still shaking off a slump — for a reason.

"I think he can hopefully pull them together," Steinbrenner said in a telephone interview today. "I think he can give them a little spark. I just feel it's the right time to do it. People may say, 'What a time to pick.' Well, why not? He represents all that is good about a leader. I'm a great believer in history, and I look at all the other leaders down through Yankee history, and Jeter is right there with them."

Jeter became the 11th captain — Lou Gehrig and Thurman Munson are among the others — and the first since Don Mattingly retired after the 1995 season. Steinbrenner discussed the appointment with Jeter last weekend in Detroit and again this morning. "He just says he wants me to be a leader, like I have been," Jeter said. "The impression I got is just continue to do the things I've been doing."

Steinbrenner was not ready to make the appointment over the winter, when a question about it prompted his famous rant about Jeter's supposed lack of focus. Jeter's measured response to the criticism made an impression on Steinbrenner, who thinks Jeter can help Manager Joe Torre as a leader.

"He's a young man that's handled it very well," Steinbrenner said. "He said what he thought. He's always available, ready to face the questions, win or lose. I think he can be a big help to Joe Torre. I think he and Joe will work great together."

Steinbrenner has expressed doubt about the effectiveness of Torre's coaching staff and has had almost no contact with Torre this season. He did not consult him on the Jeter decision.

Torre said he did not want to play down Jeter's honor but did not think Jeter could help him do his job better.

"I don't see my job being any different, as far as helping," Torre said, "because I don't know what he could tell someone if they have a question to ask me. It can't be a negative, but I don't think players are going to listen to him more now that he's captain. He's always had that respect."

Jeter is able to get his message across in private conversations and group settings, said catcher Jorge Posada, who has long considered him the captain. "When he needs to talk, people are going to listen," Posada said.

Steinbrenner clearly places great emphasis on the captaincy. He sent two of his general partners, his son Hal and his son-in-law Steve Swindal, for the announcement, as well as General Manager Brian Cashman, whose wife is due to deliver the couple's second child any day.

Posada was among those puzzled by the timing of the announcement. "Why Cincinnati?" he said. "Why not do it in New York?" Cashman was asked that at a news conference.

"This is something he's thought about for a period of time, and he made his decision," Cashman said, referring to Steinbrenner. "Is it something he was going to sit on and wait until we came home, or go forward with? The reality in that clubhouse is, informally, people recognized him as probably the captain anyway. Now the Boss has recognized him in a formal way, and that's a great honor."

It is also a great responsibility, one that could put Jeter, even without a C on his jersey, in Steinbrenner's sights when things go wrong.

Jeter dismissed that idea.

"I don't see how it would," Jeter told reporters. "I talk to you guys every day."

But dealing with the news media is just one aspect of Jeter's new role. Steinbrenner is putting his faith in Jeter, and that always carries significant demands. In the statement the team released, Steinbrenner used his favorite quotation from Gen. Douglas MacArthur: "There is no substitute for victory."

Cajoling his teammates to victory will clearly be a mandate for Jeter.

"You do what your gut tells you," Steinbrenner said. "My gut tells me this would be a good time for Derek Jeter to assume leadership. He is a great leader by the way he performs and plays. I told him I want him to be the type of cavalry officer who can sit in the saddle. You can't be a leader unless you sit in the saddle. I think he can."

Tyler Kepner

Derek Jeter, Yankees
captain, *March 28, 2007.*
Photo: Chip Litherland for
The New York Times

"I think he's the consummate professional.
He accepts things very well. I've always felt the
strength of a person's character is their ability
to accept both success and failure, without
letting either one affect you. I've watched, and
he's done that. He's a great competitor and he
can make big plays for you, but his demeanor
is always the same."

JOHN WOODEN, 95, the renowned former basketball coach for U.C.L.A., on Derek Jeter,
during a visit to the Yankees' clubhouse to see Manager Joe Torre, *Aug. 27, 2006*

Jeter's Secret? Simple: Play to Win

Aug. 18, 2006 | Derek Jeter was the host of "Saturday Night Live" in 2001, and he was nervous about it all week. He had no acting or comic background, and certainly had never performed on live television.

Jeter thought he might make a fool of himself, but the feeling subsided when he took the stage for his monologue. Everything happened so fast that 90 minutes seemed like 10. The task was remarkably easy.

"They have everything on cue cards for you," Jeter said. "So as long as you can read, you can do it."

For all of Jeter's skills, the most useful is his ability to boil down any job to its essence. In a Yankees season marked by injuries to big hitters and the mystifying mind games of Alex Rodriguez, Jeter's simple approach has stood out more than ever.

"I think that's where people get in trouble, when they start complicating things," Jeter said. "It's really not that complicated. You're playing a game where you fail more than you succeed. You've got to try to keep it as simple as possible."

Jeter has often been hailed for his intangibles, the kind of praise that can come off as a way to excuse his numbers. But this season, especially, Jeter has no need to apologize.

With a .338 average, he is second in the American League to Minnesota's Joe Mauer. He has the best on-base percentage on the Yankees, at .415. Jeter is hitting .373 with runners in scoring position.

"He may drag bunt one time, and the next time he might try to drive it out of the field on you," Baltimore Orioles catcher Chris Widger said. "It's hard, because there's no one way to pitch him to get him out. He's one of those rare guys that could bat leadoff or bat third, and he could be very successful anywhere because he'll adapt his game to whatever the team needs for him to do."

"It's simple if you look at it as: Try to win," Jeter said. "That's the bottom line. If you win, everybody benefits. It's not like, 'I won, I lost.' It's, 'We won, we lost.' That's the only way I've thought about it."

Jeter talks like this all the time. He says he knows reporters get tired of boring answers, but sometimes there is nothing much to say. He responds politely to questions, but objects to the premise of most.

"People say, 'Are you more motivated now because you lost?' " Jeter said, referring to the Yankees' years without a title. "How could you be more motivated if you want to win all the time? You're not extra-motivated. It's the same thing."

Jeter helped create the Yankees' modern mentality, in which only championship seasons are considered a success. It is an all-or-nothing mind-set that, for some, creates a joyless, pressurized environment.

But for Jeter, it is simply a fact. Every team wants to win as often as possible, so the goal must be a title every season. It is not like this everywhere, but for Jeter, it would be.

"I don't know what it would be like, but I wouldn't change," he said. "Now don't get me wrong, I do understand it's a game of numbers and people are going to pay attention to your numbers, say you did this or did that. I would love to hit .400. That would be a lot better than .200. You take pride in how you play. But that shouldn't be your main focus. Your main focus should be whether you win or lose."

Tyler Kepner

Whether it's a home run, a single the other way or even a bunt, Jeter will do whatever's needed for the team to win.
Photo: Barton Silverman,
The New York Times

Public Figure, Private Leader

April 1, 2007 | From his first spring training as the Yankees' manager, in 1996, Joe Torre knew that Derek Jeter gets it. The front office had decided that Jeter, then a rookie, would be the Yankees' starting shortstop. Torre anointed him as such to the news media. Then he read what Jeter said.

"Derek answered the same question better than I did, because he said, 'I'm going to get an opportunity to become the shortstop,'" Torre said. "And that little thing, it may have been a throwaway line for other people, but I thought: 'You know what? You're right.' In his mind, he had to earn the right to be the shortstop. In mine, I was giving him the right to be the shortstop. It's different. That impressed me."

Jeter was 21 years old then, but he quickly emerged as a leader on a veteran team that would win the World Series. Seven years later, George Steinbrenner, the Yankees' principal owner, named him captain.

ne night during spring training this year, the veterans had been removed from a game and were eager to leave Legends Field. They were off the next day, the only day off for the team during camp. But there was running to do, and Jeter made them do it.

"None of us wanted to go, and he's like, 'Let's go,'" Johnny Damon said. "He makes sure we get our work in. That's why he's him."

A crucial component of leadership, Torre said, is that those being led cannot resent the leader. On a team of veterans, the players tacitly accept Jeter's status. He is a link to the title teams of the late 1990s, he plays the game correctly and he does not betray their confidence.

"He's very private about what he does," said Jorge Posada, adding that Jeter never shares details of meetings. "That's not the way you lead."

The pitching coach Ron Guidry was a captain of the Yankees at the end of his career. He said a captain must read the personality of each player, knowing when to cajole and when to coddle.

"The team captain is a friendly shoulder," Guidry said. "He's the guy you want to come talk to you, unless you go and talk to him first."

Jeter probably conducts more interviews with reporters than any other Yankee. He pitches video games and Gatorade, and he dates celebrities. Yet there is much about him that fans do not know, and that extends to his role in the clubhouse.

"A lot of the things that Derek does go unseen," Jason Giambi said. "He does talk to guys on the side, but he doesn't make it a media thing."

Jeter said he felt responsible for answering questions about games and for representing the Yankees in public. He knows he has an image as a quiet leader who rarely speaks up, and it seems to amuse him.

There is much about his captain's role he leaves unsaid, and that is how he wants it.

"I always find it interesting when people say, 'Well, he's a lead-by-example guy, he doesn't ever say anything,'" Jeter said. "How do you know? I don't do things through the media, but that doesn't mean I don't say things or I'm not vocal. You guys maybe don't know about it. But you don't have to know about everything."

Torre would probably approve of that comment, too.

Tyler Kepner

Since 1995, with only very rare and brief exceptions, Yankees fans have shown complete support for Derek Jeter.
Photo: Barton Silverman, The New York Times

Jeter makes himself readily
available to the media
and is always honest —
but also discreet.
Photo: Richard Perry,
The New York Times

"You know, a lot of people say he's a quiet captain, and maybe he is, but he's a guy that leads by example, and that's the kind of guy I want to follow."

BRETT GARDNER, rookie Yankees outfielder, on Derek Jeter, *Sept. 23, 2008*

The "greatest fans in the world" salute Derek Jeter after he passes Lou Gehrig and sets a new record for most career hits by a Yankee, *Sept. 11, 2009.*
Photo: Richard Perry, The New York Times

"We're relying on you to take the memories from this Stadium, add them to the new memories that come at the new Yankee Stadium, and continue to pass them on from generation to generation. So on behalf of the entire organization, we just want to take this moment to salute you, the greatest fans in the world."

DEREK JETER, *Sept. 22, 2008*

CHAPTER ⑧

LEGEND

Derek Jeter closed the original Yankee Stadium in 2008 with stirring words to the fans, urging them to take their memories across the street and help the team create new ones. The fans needed inspiration; the Yankees were finishing a season without a playoff appearance for the first time in Jeter's career.

The task of spokesman fell naturally to Jeter, the team captain who had more hits in the old shrine than anybody. But the elder statesman's status did not portend a decline in Jeter's skills. There was plenty of life left in his career, and he proved it with one of his best seasons in 2009: 18 home runs, 30 steals and a .334 average. Then he helped christen the new Yankee Stadium with another World Series title.

That meant a fifth championship ring and a fifth ride up Broadway on a crisp fall day with confetti falling from the sky. The victory capped a remarkable run for Jeter, who in September had broken Lou Gehrig's franchise record for hits. He smacked the milestone single to right field, a classic Jeter hit, another on his march to 3,000 — and beyond.

Pinstriped for Greatness

March 21, 1999 | It is a testament to Derek Jeter that his peers will project his future greatness, estimate how big a star he will become or try to guess what his place in history will be. Baseball veterans typically frown on such conjecture, for their game is relentlessly demanding and challenging and they know almost all young players will wilt.

But peers are sure Jeter will be exceptional for a long, long time. The Yankees' shortstop has averaged nearly 200 hits per season. He has finished third in the Most Valuable Player balloting. He is among the game's most popular players. He is only 24 years old.

What will he be when he's 35? "An unbelievable star," said Darryl Strawberry. "He could be as big as Michael Jordan, because he's got a level head, he's a good kid, he knows how to play the game, he's not afraid, he's not intimidated and he's handsome as ever. And he's in New York."

Said Paul O'Neill: "He has a chance to be a Hall of Fame player. He's got that much time in his career, and that much talent."

That much talent, in all those things that make a star.

Hitting

Tony Gwynn, the eight-time batting champion from the San Diego Padres, had a moment to pause at second base during the postseason last year and turned to Jeter. "You just keep doing what you do," Gwynn said.

Gwynn believes that Jeter has a terrific approach at the plate, that inside-out swing that allows Jeter to smash the ball through the right side or up the middle, with results. He averaged 192 hits a season in his first three full seasons, and clearly is improving — he had 203 hits in only 149 games in 1998, batting .324. If Jeter remains healthy and plays another 14 seasons, averaging 190 hits a year, he would finish his career with approximately 3,250 hits.

Power

Jeter is not muscular like Jose Canseco or Mark McGwire; he doesn't have the steel-mill chest. But he is very strong — last year, Jeter became the first right-handed hitter in the history of Yankee Stadium to hit the ball in the upper deck in right field, and he and Strawberry and Bernie Williams probably hit the most home runs in batting practice.

"He doesn't realize what kind of power he has," Strawberry said. "Being a home run hitter is a natural thing, and he has the natural ability to hit home runs. He has a natural swing for becoming a 30-home run hitter. He's going to get stronger each year."

Base Running

Jeter has the quickness and the speed to steal bases, and he's gaining the requisite knowledge. Jose Cardenal, the Yankees' first base coach, thinks that as soon as Jeter acquires confidence in his base running — fearlessness — he will steal 40 to 50 a year, "or maybe more."

Jeter increased his stolen bases from 14 to 23 to 30 in his first three years, and intends to run more.

Fielding

Jeter gained the consistency the Yankees wanted from him, reducing his errors to nine last year; he did not make his first throwing error until June 20. To Kansas City Manager Tony Muser and others, Jeter already ranks among the game's best shortstops.

Last season, Jeter curbed a habit of shuffling forward and to his right slightly as a pitch was made, and he was in better position to make more plays. With greater anticipation — understanding the hitters, understanding how they will hit the ball on certain counts — the Yankees coach Willie Randolph thinks Jeter will get to more balls, to his left, in particular, and to his right.

A Future Captain

Jeter played alongside Don Mattingly for just a few weeks at the end of the 1995 season, but Mattingly left Jeter a keepsake. At a time when the Yankees held spring training in Fort Lauderdale, Fla., Jeter and Mattingly finished a workout on a back field one afternoon, all alone. Some of their teammates were playing an exhibition game, others already were done for the day, and now Mattingly and Jeter were headed back to the clubhouse, as well. The stadium was completely empty; there was nobody around — no fans, no coaches, no one except for two exhausted, sweating ballplayers.

"Let's run in," Mattingly told Jeter. "You never know who's watching."

Jeter remembers vividly how they ran back to the clubhouse, side by side, through the empty ballpark, just because it was the right thing to do.

Mattingly was a captain, perhaps the player most responsible for creating the intensely professional and respectful culture that has been cultivated in the Yankees' clubhouse — and Jeter likely will be the keeper of the flame for years to come, as Manager Joe Torre and pitcher David Cone and many others believe.

"He's not intimidated by any situation," catcher Joe Girardi said, "and to be a leader, you have to be like that. He's well respected. He's able to make light of a lot of situations, to keep guys relaxed."

Captains: Don Mattingly and Jeter, *July 8, 2007.* *Photo: Diamond Images/ Getty Images*

Star Power

Like his fellow shortstops Nomar Garciaparra and Alex Rodriguez, Jeter is already among the game's most recognizable figures, one of its symbols of excellence. "He's exactly what baseball needs, a young player, talented, who really, he communicates exactly what this sport is," said Bud Selig, baseball's commissioner.

Steve Rosner, an executive vice president for Integrated Sports International, a company that deals in marketing, says that so long as Jeter stays with the Yankees and the Yankees continue to be successful, Jeter could develop into the city's biggest Madison Avenue star "in a couple of decades, since Reggie."

"It's a remarkable start to his career," Cone said. "There's no reason to believe he can't be in the upper echelon of all-time great Yankee players."

Buster Olney

"There's no reason to believe he can't be in the upper echelon of all-time great Yankee players."

DAVID CONE, who pitched for the Yankees and other teams, evaluating Derek Jeter after three full seasons, *March 21, 1999*

▲ Hall of Fame shortstop
Phil Rizzuto goes flying
over Jackie Robinson of
the Brooklyn Dodgers —
but not before completing
the first-inning double
play in Game 6 of the
World Series, *Oct. 5, 1947.*
Photo: Associated Press

► Jeter does an
aerial split to avoid the
Cleveland Indians'
Grady Sizemore at second
base after completing
the double play against
Asdrubal Cabrera at first
in Game 1 of the division
series, *Oct. 4, 2007.*
Photo: Richard Perry,
The New York Times

Jeter is the latest in a long line of prominent Yankees shortstops. The line began with Kid Elberfeld, Jack Knight and Roger Peckinpaugh (1913 to 1921), who was a defensive star, clutch hitter and team captain. At center in this Yankee Stadium photo from 1921 (when the team won its first American League pennant), Peckinpaugh is flanked by, left to right, first baseman Wally Pipp, second-year outfielders Babe Ruth and Bob Meusel (two key members of "Murderers' Row" in the 1920's), and veteran third baseman Frank "Home Run" Baker.
Photo: Mark Rucker, Transcendental Graphics/ Getty Images

Tony Kubek tags out Roberto Clemente of the Pittsburgh Pirates during Game 1 of the World Series at Forbes Field, Oct. 5, 1960. Kubek (1958 to 1965) followed such standouts at short as Everett Scott and Mark Koenig (1920's), Frank Crosetti (1930's and early 1940's) and Phil Rizzuto (1940's to 1956). All of them — like most excellent shortstops in those decades — were highly regarded primarily for their fielding.
Photo: Robert Riger, Getty Images

Bucky Dent stops an attempted steal by Hal McRae of the Kansas City Royals in a late 1970's game at Royal Stadium. Solid defensively, Dent (1977 to 1982) is probably the best known of the many shortstops between Kubek and Jeter, mostly because of his dramatic home run against the Boston Red Sox in the one-game regular season playoff on *Oct. 2, 1978.*

Photo: Focus on Sport/Getty Images

Jeter and Rose Look at the Record

Aug. 23, 2000 | Pete Rose, Joe Morgan, Bob Gibson and Nolan Ryan, from the geriatrics set, and Derek Jeter, of the comparative kiddie corps, were taking part in a five-inning celebrity charity softball game today in the ballpark behind the Yogi Berra Museum on the campus of Montclair State University in Little Falls, N.J. Proceeds from the game benefited the Make a Wish Foundation.

Jeter sat down next to Rose on the bench. "Think you can break Pete's record?" he was asked. Rose, of course, is the career leader with 4,256 career hits.

"I doubt it," Jeter said. "You gotta play a lot of years." Jeter, it should be noted, had more hits in his first four seasons — 807 — than anyone in baseball history.

"It means nothing," he said. "You have to get 200 hits for 20 years, and you're still not there."

"You know why he won't break it?" Rose said. "Because he makes too much money.

"He'll be getting eight or nine million a year for the next few years. In 20 years, he'd have to be making $20 million a year. Nobody can afford that!"

"He's my agent," said Jeter, throwing an arm around Rose's shoulder.

Ira Berkow

With Dribbler, Jeter Reaches 2,000

May 27, 2006 | The night was damp, the Yankees' opponent was doleful, the holiday getaway traffic was dispiriting. The reason why 48,035 fans braved gloomy skies, gridlock and the Kansas City Royals last night would become as clear as an indelible memory in the bottom of the fourth inning.

Derek Jeter, the Yankees' shortstop, led off against Royals starter Scott Elarton, who had retired him on a first-pitch fly out in the first. Popping flashbulbs blazed Jeter's path from the Yankee Stadium on-deck circle to home plate, as if he were a leading man at a red-carpet premiere.

The Yankees were down by three runs and the fans were up on their feet cheering because Jeter was the one they came to see. He is No. 1 in the fans' hearts, and by the time he is finished he may be No. 1 on the Yankees' career hits list. Jeter took a notable step in that direction with a dribbler in the fourth.

Paul Bako, the Royals' catcher, fielded Jeter's ball, but his throw sailed over the head of the first baseman, Doug Mientkiewicz, and Jeter went to second. After a pause of several seconds that heightened the drama of the moment, the ruling came down: The official scorer in the press box awarded Jeter a hit and charged Bako with an error. That is how Jeter became the eighth Yankee to reach 2,000 hits, joining Lou Gehrig, Babe Ruth, Mickey Mantle, Bernie Williams, Joe DiMaggio, Don Mattingly and Yogi Berra.

Jeter's parents, Dorothy and Charles, were in the stands. As the official scorer deliberated, a television camera caught Jeter's mother mouthing to his father that the play was an "error."

"It's a good thing she wasn't scoring," said Jeter, who also singled in the seventh to finish 2 for 3 with two walks.

"Two thousand hits, 31 years old," Manager Joe Torre said. "That's not bad. It's pretty impressive how consistent he has been for 10 years. Everybody is hoping he stays healthy, so he can get to that next level."

In the home dugout, the players draped themselves over the railing like bunting and applauded Jeter's achievement. From their vantage point, his accomplishment looked less like a milestone than a stepping-stone toward what is considered perhaps his destiny: becoming the first player to reach 3,000 hits as a Yankee.

"Oh yeah, he can get to 3,000," said Bernie Williams, the right fielder who recorded his 2,000th hit in 2004. "He's still has a lot of career ahead of him, you know. He's just breezing through this."

Karen Crouse

A Good Start

Aug. 30, 1999 | With his two singles yesterday in the Yankees' 11-5 victory over the Seattle Mariners, Derek Jeter has more hits in the first four full years of his career, 751 (he also had 12 in 1995), than hitters like Ted Williams (749 in his first four seasons), Cal Ripken (745), Lou Gehrig (736), Ty Cobb (729), Pete Rose (723) and Henry Aaron (718) had.

"I look around when I was at the All-Star Game to see if he's got anything I don't like. I said, 'Man, you're the perfect man.' Too bad I don't have a daughter. He's the best thing ever in the game. He's got everything you want. Who's better than Derek Jeter? Nobody in the game."

OZZIE GUILLEN, manager of the Chicago White Sox, on Derek Jeter, *April 24, 2008*

After permanently breaking Lou Gehrig's record for most career hits at Yankee Stadium, Jeter raises his batting helmet in a show of appreciation to the fans. *Photo: Barton Silverman, The New York Times*

Yanks Fall, But Jeter Continues His Climb

Sept. 17, 2008 | With one crisp swing on the first pitch of his first at-bat, Derek Jeter slapped a ground ball under Juan Uribe's glove and into left field to break Lou Gehrig's 71-year-old record for most hits at Yankee Stadium.

Though there might have been a case for scoring the play an error, few among the 52,558 fans would complain about Jeter's 1,270th hit in the Bronx. Even if the play was ruled an error, fans would have only had to wait until the fifth inning, when he again singled during a 6-2 loss to the White Sox.

"It's kind of hard to enjoy because we lost the game," Jeter said. "But I definitely appreciate everything the fans have done."

Jeter was greeted at first base by the capacity crowd on its feet and a supernova of flashbulbs. After a moment of apparent hesitation, Jeter doffed his helmet.

Jeter has spent his entire 14-year career with the Yankees and took 81 fewer home games than Gehrig to break his record. It is one of the few marks that is guaranteed never to be surpassed since the Stadium, where Gehrig made his debut in 1923, will close after Sunday's game.

Joshua Robinson

"What I was thinking as Derek was speaking was that it was going to be one of those moments that will play over and over for the next 100 years, like Lou Gehrig, how it doesn't happen very often that an individual Yankee gets to address the entire Stadium on an occasion this special. And no doubt it had to be Derek."

GENERAL MANAGER BRIAN CASHMAN, *Sept. 23, 2008*

Yankee Stadium's Closing Night

Sept. 22, 2008 | On Sunday night in the Bronx, Yankee Stadium hosted a baseball game for the last time. It went out the way it opened, with a victory, this one by 7-3 over the Baltimore Orioles. Babe Ruth hit the first home run, in 1923, and Jose Molina hit the last, a two-run shot to left in the fourth inning.

More than 20 former Yankees returned for the pregame ceremonies.

Derek Jeter's parents and sister joined him on the field before the first pitch, as two of George Steinbrenner's children presented him with a crystal bat for breaking Gehrig's record for hits at the Stadium.

Jeter would get no more hits on Sunday, going 0 for 5, but he went down as the last Yankee ever to bat at Yankee Stadium, with a groundout to third in the eighth inning.

Tyler Kepner

Jeter Thanks Fans in Speech after Game

Sept. 22, 2008 | The last game at Yankee Stadium was over, but the fans waited. There would never be another pitch thrown in this beautiful park, but the fans still waited. That was when Derek Jeter gathered his Yankees teammates, walked to the pitcher's mound, took a microphone and thanked them.

Jeter told the fans that it was an honor for the players to wear the Yankee uniform. Applause. He said the Yankees were about history, tradition and memories, and passing along the memories. Even more applause. Then Jeter told the last 54,610 people to sit in these blue seats that they were the greatest fans in the world. Deafening applause.

"I was scared to death," Jeter said. "When I was younger, I used to get nervous when I had to do an oral report in front of 25 people. I guess I've come a long way."

A few days ago, the Yankees asked Jeter, the team captain, if he would address the fans after Sunday's game. Jeter agreed, but he said he did not learn until before the game that he would actually be speaking. Manager Joe Girardi removed Jeter with two outs in the ninth inning so he could receive one final ovation.

"Two outs in the ninth, I thought, 'I better think of something,'" Jeter said.

Even though Jeter was offering his words to more than 54,000 fans, he did not prepare.

"I didn't think about it," Jeter said. "I didn't know what I was going to say. I know I wanted to acknowledge the fans. If you ask me now what I said, I probably couldn't tell you."

But Jeter's words worked. Like Jeter's play, his speech was effective and classy.

"Derek said it with such eloquent words when he thanked the fans for their support," said Bernie Williams, the former Yankee who received the loudest pregame ovation.

After Jeter's speech, he led the Yankees on a lap around the Stadium in which the players thanked the fans some more. Because police officers in riot gear and officers on horseback were stationed around the Stadium, the players remained about 50 feet away from the fans. Still, it was a nice ending to the last night at the Stadium.

"This was perfect," Jeter said. "I don't know if I could use another adjective. It was perfect."

Jack Curry

Jeter pays tribute to
Yankees tradition and fans
on the last night of the
original Yankee Stadium,
Sept. 21, 2008.
Photo: Vincent Laforet for
The New York Times

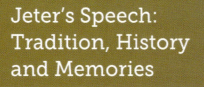

Jeter's Speech: Tradition, History and Memories

"For all of us up here, it's a huge honor to put this uniform on every day and come out here and play. And every member of this organization, past and present, has been calling this place home for 85 years. There's a lot of tradition, a lot of history and a lot of memories. Now, the great thing about memories is you're able to pass it along from generation to generation. And although things are going to change next year, we're going to move across the street, there are a few things with the New York Yankees that never change — that's pride, it's tradition, and most of all, we have the greatest fans in the world.

"We're relying on you to take the memories from this Stadium, add them to the new memories that come at the new Yankee Stadium, and continue to pass them on from generation to generation. So on behalf of the entire organization, we just want to take this moment to salute you, the greatest fans in the world."

Jeter has joined the ranks of Yankees giants, including Hall of Famers Mickey Mantle (right), Lou Gehrig and Joe DiMaggio (both opposite, flanked by catcher Bill Dickey and second baseman Tony Lazzeri, who are also in the Hall of Fame). *Photos: Larry C. Morris, The New York Times (right); Associated Press (opposite)*

Jeter Is Approaching Gehrig with a Sense of the Moment

Sept. 3, 2009 | The records are piling up for Derek Jeter, and the more he hits, the quicker they come. Most hits at the original Yankee Stadium. Most hits by a shortstop. Most hits in the history of the Yankees.

The last mark still belongs to Lou Gehrig, at least for a few more days. Gehrig had 2,721 hits. Jeter, who had a hit Wednesday against the Orioles, has 2,713. Individual records can be awkward for Jeter, who insists that winning is all that matters. But he said he would appreciate this one.

"I was talking to my parents not too long ago, and they were telling me, 'You've got to learn to enjoy some of these things as they're happening — there's nothing wrong with that,'" Jeter said. "So I'm sure it's something that I'll enjoy if it happens."

Barring injury, the question for Jeter is not if, but how soon. He had 46 hits in August, his most in a calendar month since August 1998. He is batting .369 since June 25, the day before his 35th birthday.

Catcher Jorge Posada marveled at the names Jeter has passed on the hits list — Ruth and DiMaggio, Mantle and Berra, Mattingly and Williams — but said Jeter had never discussed it with him. Yet because it is a Yankees record, and not merely a round number signifying individual greatness, Jeter said it would have extra meaning.

Along the way, Jeter has absorbed the team's history. The shadow of Gehrig is hard to miss.

"I just know how he carried himself, how he was respected," Jeter said. "He went out there, he played every day and he was consistent. Those are all the things that I think players strive to be."

The workaday ethos is part of the legacy of Gehrig, who played 2,130 consecutive games before A.L.S. ended his career. It is also important to Jeter, the major league leader in games played since 1996.

The torrid month has put him close to a record Jeter will cherish, if he takes his parents' advice.

Tyler Kepner

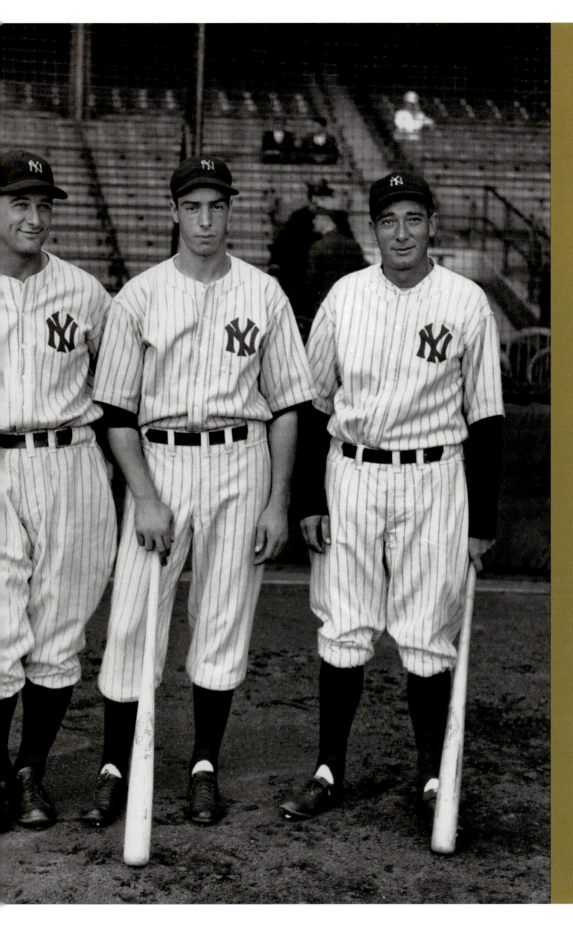

Career Hits

Jeter moved past a series of legends en route to the record for hits by a Yankee. Here are their own previous rankings and hit totals, along with date and opposing team when Jeter passed each one.

7 Yogi Berra
2,148
Sept. 30, 2006
(vs. Toronto Blue Jays)

6 Don Mattingly
2,153
April 6, 2007
(vs. Baltimore Orioles)

5 Joe DiMaggio
2,214
May 23, 2007
(vs. Boston Red Sox)

4 Bernie Williams
2,336
Sept. 17, 2007
(vs. Orioles)

3 Mickey Mantle
2,415
June 4, 2008
(vs. Blue Jays)

2 Babe Ruth
2,518
Sept. 9, 2008
(vs. Los Angeles Angels)

1 Lou Gehrig
2,721
Sept. 11, 2009
(vs. Orioles)

Already weakened by his as-yet-undiagnosed fatal disease, Lou Gehrig grounds into a double play in an exhibition game against the Brooklyn Dodgers at Ebbets Field, April 18, 1939. Twelve days later, the Iron Horse would play in his 2,130th and final game, before benching himself on May 2.
Photo: Mark Rucker, Transcendental Graphics/Getty Images

Derek Jeter breaks
Lou Gehrig's record for
career hits by a Yankee,
Sept. 11, 2009.
Photo: Richard Perry,
The New York Times

Jeter Passes Gehrig as Yankees Hits Leader

Sept. 12, 2009 | Derek Jeter grew up on Yankees history, by birth and by providence. He was nurtured as a fan by his grandmother, who lived in New Jersey, and drafted into the tradition as a first-round pick in 1992. Only recently, though, did Jeter learn that nobody had gathered 3,000 hits for his team.

Teammates stumbled on the fact while paging through a record book, and Jeter said they wondered who had the most. The record was clearly in Jeter's sights, but he never resolved to target Lou Gehrig, never made it a goal.

"I never imagined, I never dreamt of this," Jeter said after midnight Saturday morning. "Your dream was always to play for the team. Once you get here, you just want to stay and try to be consistent. So this really wasn't a part of it. The whole experience has been overwhelming."

On a drizzly Friday night at Yankee Stadium, Jeter's graceful grind through 15 seasons vaulted him past Gehrig, his storied predecessor as team captain. Gehrig held the record for more than 70 years, until Jeter's 2,722nd hit skipped past Gehrig's old position, first base, for a single.

Jeter connected in the third inning of a 10-4 loss to the Baltimore Orioles that was delayed at the start and again in the seventh inning. Jeter lashed a 2-0 fastball from Chris Tillman on a hop past the diving first baseman, Luke Scott. The hard-hit ball to opposite field is Jeter's signature hit, and he spread his arms wide and clapped after rounding first base.

The players on the Yankees' bench poured from the dugout to greet him, taking turns giving hugs. Alex Rodriguez was the first to arrive, before Robinson Cano, Mark Teixeira, Joba Chamberlain and the rest.

"I think you saw the closeness of the group," Manager Joe Girardi said. "Even the guys that have only been here for a year, they understood."

The fans chanted Jeter's first and last names, and Jeter waved his helmet to all corners of the new Yankee Stadium. As he did on Wednesday, when he tied the record, Jeter pointed to the box with his parents, sister and friends on the suite level above the Yankees' on-deck circle. Jeter's girlfriend, the actress Minka Kelly, stood beside his mother, Dorothy, and both smiled widely.

The crowd continued to chant for Jeter, and Nick Swisher, the next batter, stepped out of the box to make the moment last. As the cheers cascaded over Jeter, he waved his helmet again and then clapped a few times in Swisher's direction: back to work.

"The fans," Jeter said, when asked what he would remember most, years from now. "It wasn't ideal conditions tonight, and for the fans to stick around, it really means a lot. Since day one, they've always been very supportive. They're just as much a part of this as I am."

The hit arrived in Jeter's second at-bat against Tillman, a heralded Orioles rookie who challenged him with a 94-mile-an-hour pitch. Tillman had won their duel in the first inning, striking Jeter out with a curveball after getting ahead with fastballs.

It was raining then, a persistent, heavy mist swirling around the stadium, with standing pools of water on the warning track. In the third inning, though, the rain tapered for a bit. In any case, the crowd of 46,771 did not seem to care. The fans stood for Jeter then, snapping photos of each pitch, and an inning later, commemorative T-shirts and pennants were on sale at stadium gift shops.

Principal owner George Steinbrenner was not there — his health has declined, and he has not been to a home game since opening day. But his publicist quickly issued a statement on his behalf.

"For those who say today's game can't produce legendary players, I have two words: Derek Jeter," Steinbrenner's statement said. "As historic and significant as becoming the Yankees' all-time hit leader is, the accomplishment is all the more impressive because Derek is one of the finest young men playing the game today."

Jeter said Steinbrenner called him during the second rain delay, and that Steinbrenner had nice things to say. Jeter is a link to the owner's more visible, vigorous days, and he seemed touched that Steinbrenner reached out.

"You miss seeing him around here as much as you used to," Jeter said. "But it was great to hear his voice."

Steinbrenner's statement went on to praise the character and ability of Jeter, comparing him favorably to Gehrig, who died of A.L.S. in 1941, a little more than two years after his final hit. Gehrig was far more prolific as a run producer, but Jeter matched his hit total Wednesday in just 64 fewer plate appearances.

He broke the record with the Yankees comfortably ahead in the division, with a clear path to the playoffs and few pressing team issues. The last few days, then, have played out as a sort of Derek Jeter Appreciation Week for fans and teammates.

During the second delay, of 67 minutes, Girardi sent the regulars home before the game concluded. They appeared in the interview room before leaving, Andy Pettitte, Rodriguez and Jorge Posada sitting at a podium, swapping stories about their teammate and friend.

Pettitte and Posada were second-year professionals in 1992, when Jeter joined their Class A team in Greensboro, N.C., late in the season. Jeter made nine errors in 11 games and hit .243. He was skinny then, and raw as a fielder. But something stood out.

"We were so young and started this run off at such a young age, and you knew that he was special," Pettitte said. "You knew that he carried himself a little bit different than a lot of other guys, a lot of class, a lot of charisma, a lot of confidence for as young as he was."

Rodriguez and Jeter have had a complicated relationship, like Gehrig and Babe Ruth in their day. But Rodriguez was gracious, calling Jeter the ultimate winner who continues to improve. Jeter is hitting .331.

"I don't think he's ever played any better than he's playing right now, which is awesome," Rodriguez said. "He's running really well, he's playing great defense, he's hitting, he's hitting for power. Where he takes it from now, we're all having fun watching him."

The possibilities were underscored by this oddity: Jeter reached his milestone exactly 24 years after Pete Rose passed Ty Cobb as baseball's career hits leader. Jeter, 35, has more hits than Rose did at the same age. Rose played until age 45 and finished with 4,256 hits.

That chase, if Jeter pursues it, is far off. For now, Jeter said, passing Gehrig is his finest individual accomplishment.

"I can't think of anything else that stands out more so, and I say that because of the person that I was able to pass," Jeter said. "Lou Gehrig, being a former captain and what he stood for, you mention his name to any baseball fan around the country, it means a lot."

Jeter's name holds a similar meaning in the modern game, which he is in no hurry to leave. Jeter is signed through next season and said this week he would keep playing as long as he has fun.

The game is exhilarating now for Jeter, with the Yankees 40 games over .500 and possessing, perhaps, their best chance for a title in years. He has helped carry them with a storm of hits, 188 this season, part of an annual barrage that has set a new standard for the most famous team in sports.

Tyler Kepner

A fan at Yankee Stadium reacts to Jeter's record-setting single.
Photo: Richard Perry, The New York Times

Applause Is Appropriate Response

Sept. 12, 2009 | Clap hands for Derek Jeter.

Clap hands, the way he does when he pulls into second base in the bottom of the ninth, staring into the dugout with that grin of his.

Clap hands for Derek Jeter, breaking the record of Lou Gehrig for most hits by a Yankee. Not just any franchise. The Yankees.

Clap hands for Jeter, who is having the year of his life, swatting base hits and fielding his position, not that he will talk much about himself.

Raised right, the other day he said his parents gave him permission to put aside his captain persona and, for a second or two, enjoy approaching Gehrig's record.

The record is important because the Yankees are — and recognize that this is coming from an old Brooklyn Dodgers fan — the great sports franchise of America, in terms of championships and legends, never mind the Steelers and the Celtics and so on.

Jeter now has more hits as a Yankee than Ruth or Gehrig or DiMaggio or Mantle or Mattingly or Williams, all those grand Yankees who need no introduction. He has surpassed them in the summer he turned 35, still metaphorically diving into the stands, chin-first.

Women of all ages love Derek Jeter. Ruth Taxerman of New Jersey, who died Aug. 28, saw Gehrig play when she was young, and said he was very handsome, and she thought the same about Jeter. In her final days, the radio was on in her room, so she could follow her surrogate sons. She told her actual son, Alan Taxerman, that Jeter was the perfect Yankee to break Gehrig's record.

Jeter has accomplished this feat in his prime, not backing into it, some grand old man playing a few days a week, designated hitter, backup first baseman, the stuff of old age, way down the pike. He breaks the record lean and spry and relatively healthy, although how would anybody know? Joe Torre — Mr. Torre — would ask how he felt, and Jeter would say, "I'm fine." Tells that to the trainers, too.

The captain breaks the record at home in what figures to be another pleasant Yankee autumn. The World Series ends in November this year. Ever since a few minutes past mid-

Jeter heads for first base and another entry in the record books.
Photo: Richard Perry, The New York Times

night in 2001, Jeter's nom de baseball has been Mr. November.

The postseason is usually a crapshoot. Records involve a certain amount of luck, too. The other great Yankees had their asterisks, so to speak. Ruth was mostly a pitcher until he came to the Yankees. Gehrig was felled by a merciless disease. DiMaggio missed three seasons in the service and burned out before his time. Mantle was hurt, and sometimes was not at his best for other reasons. Mattingly hurt his back and then retired young to try to hold his family together. Williams had a slow start before Torre arrived in 1996 and figured out the sensitive young man could play.

or that matter, Jeter could have more hits than he does. He played 15 games in 1995, filling in for the injured Tony Fernandez, and everybody could see he was a winner, but the organization had its game plan. If it had played Jeter, the Yankees might have beaten the Mariners — unless the Mariners had intuitively used their own marvelous kid, Alex Rodriguez.

Clap hands for Derek Jeter's four subsequent rings. Clap hands for the fluke home run in 1996 that a young fan misdirected from the right-fielder's glove. Clap hands for Jeter's home run in Shea Stadium in the 2000 Series. Clap hands for 2001, when Jeter materialized near the first-base on-deck circle to corral a wayward ball and flip it home to get Jeremy Giambi, who never bothered to slide, Jeremy, slide. Clap hands for Jeter's dive into the third-base stands in 2004, bloodying his chin. Clap hands for the double off Pedro Martinez in 2003 and the green-eyed stare into the Yankee dugout, as if to say, You, too, guys!

Jeter leads by example. When prodded by reporters about some temporary flareup, Jeter fixes those green eyes on the interrogator and says, how do you know what goes on behind the closed doors?

Only rarely does he send a message. In 2002, the team was missing Tino and Scotty and Paulie, had too many transients, yet writers suggested the Yankees had championship experience. "Some of us have," Jeter said. He sizzled slightly when one Yankee or another was connected to drugs. Not all of us do that, Jeter would say.

For all this, we really do not know Derek Jeter, except by the respectful way he refers to his father and mother and sister. He is single and appears to go out with lovely women, but he seems to be discreet, and amen to that.

We don't know what he thinks about politics or religion or current events. He sells cars on television — including the commercial in which he insists he is just a salesman, not a shortstop, but the kid susses him out.

He has set the tone for the Yankees, on the field and off. And in the summer he turned 35, he has broken the franchise record for hits, and we all get to watch him play. Clap hands for that.

George Vecsey

"For those who say today's game can't produce legendary players, I have two words: Derek Jeter."

GEORGE STEINBRENNER, in a statement issued after Jeter's record-breaking single, *Sept. 12, 2009*

◀ Jeter welcomes, left to right, the first lady, Michelle Obama; Hall of Fame catcher Yogi Berra; and the vice president's wife, Dr. Jill Biden, to the pitcher's mound at Yankee Stadium for the ceremonial first pitch before Game 1 of the World Series, *Oct. 28, 2009.*
Photo: Chang W. Lee,
The New York Times

▼ President Barack Obama speaks to Derek Jeter during a White House ceremony honoring the 2009 world champions, the New York Yankees, *April 26, 2010.*
Photo: Saul Loeb, Agence France-Presse/Getty Images

The Texas Rangers
bat in the sixth inning
of Game 5 of the
championship series with
the Yankees as the sun
sets over Yankee Stadium,
Oct. 20, 2010.
Photo: Chang W. Lee,
The New York Times

On polished diamonds and makeshift fields, youngsters like Chris Herrera, at Van Cortlandt Park in the Bronx, play the game of baseball — and carry on the dreams that Derek Jeter had when he was a boy.
Photo: James Estrin, The New York Times

Derek Sanderson Jeter

Born: June 26, 1974
Shortstop, no. 2
Bats: Right
Throws: Right
Drafted (New York Yankees): June 1, 1992
Signed: June 27, 1992

MINOR LEAGUES

1992: Yankees, Gulf Coast League (Rookie class), 47 games, .202, 12 errors (.943)
1992: Greensboro Hornets, South Atlantic League (A), 11 games, .243, 9 errors (.813)
1993: Hornets, 128 games, .295, 56 errors (.889)
1994: Tampa Yankees, Florida State League (A), 69 games, .329, 12 errors (.961)
1994: Albany-Colonie Yankees, Eastern League (AA), 34 games, .377, 6 errors (.961)
1994: Columbus Clippers, International League (AAA), 35 games, .349, 7 errors (.955)
1995: Clippers, 123 games, .317, 29 errors (.953)

Major league debut: May 29, 1995

KEY:			
G	games	**SB**	stolen bases
AB	at-bats	**OBP**	on-base percentage
R	runs	**SLG**	slugging percentage
H	hits	**BA**	batting average
2B	doubles	**TC**	total chances
3B	triples	**PO**	putouts
HR	home runs	**A**	assists
RBI	runs batted in	**E**	errors
TB	total bases	**DP**	double plays
BB	bases on balls	**FPCT**	fielding percentage
SO	strikeouts		

BATTING, REGULAR SEASON

SEASON	G	AB	R	H	2B	3B	HR	RBI	TB	BB	SO	SB	OBP	SLG	BA
1995	15	48	5	12	4	1	0	7	18	3	11	0	.294	.375	.250
1996	157	582	104	183	25	6	10	78	250	48	102	14	.370	.430	.314
1997	159	654	116	190	31	7	10	70	265	74	125	23	.370	.405	.291
1998	149	626	127	203	25	8	19	84	301	57	119	30	.384	.481	.324
1999	158	627	134	219	37	9	24	102	346	91	116	19	.438	.552	.349
2000	148	593	119	201	31	4	15	73	285	68	99	22	.416	.481	.339
2001	150	614	110	191	35	3	21	74	295	56	99	27	.377	.480	.311
2002	157	644	124	191	26	0	18	75	271	73	114	32	.373	.421	.297
2003	119	482	87	156	25	3	10	52	217	43	88	11	.393	.450	.324
2004	154	643	111	188	44	1	23	78	303	46	99	23	.352	.471	.292
2005	159	654	122	202	25	5	19	70	294	77	117	14	.389	.450	.309
2006	154	623	118	214	39	3	14	97	301	69	102	34	.417	.483	.343
2007	156	639	102	206	39	4	12	73	289	56	100	15	.388	.452	.322
2008	150	596	88	179	25	3	11	69	243	52	85	11	.363	.408	.300
2009	153	634	107	212	27	1	18	66	295	72	90	30	.406	.465	.334
2010	157	663	111	179	30	3	10	67	245	63	106	18	.340	.370	.270
Career	2295	9322	1685	2926	468	61	234	1135	4218	948	1572	323	.385	.452	.314

BATTING, POSTSEASON

YR	SERIES	OPP	G	AB	R	H	2B	3B	HR	RBI	TB	BB	SO	SB	OBP	SLG	BA
1996	ALDS	TEX	4	17	2	7	1	0	0	1	8	0	2	0	.412	.471	.412
1996	ALCS	BAL	5	24	5	10	2	0	1	1	15	0	5	2	.417	.625	.417
1996	WS	ATL	6	20	5	5	0	0	0	1	5	4	6	1	.400	.250	.250
1997	ALDS	CLE	5	21	6	7	1	0	2	2	14	3	5	1	.417	.667	.333
1998	ALDS	TEX	3	9	0	1	0	0	0	0	1	2	2	0	.273	.111	.111
1998	ALCS	CLE	6	25	3	5	1	1	0	2	8	2	5	3	.259	.320	.200
1998	WS	SD	4	17	4	6	0	0	0	1	6	3	3	0	.450	.353	.353
1999	ALDS	TEX	3	11	3	5	1	1	0	0	8	2	3	0	.538	.727	.455
1999	ALCS	BOS	5	20	3	7	1	0	1	3	11	2	3	0	.409	.550	.350
1999	WS	ATL	4	17	4	6	1	0	0	1	7	1	3	3	.389	.412	.353
2000	ALDS	OAK	5	19	1	4	0	0	0	2	4	2	3	0	.318	.211	.211
2000	ALCS	SEA	6	22	6	7	0	0	2	5	13	6	7	1	.464	.591	.318
2000	WS	NYM	5	22	6	9	2	1	2	2	19	3	8	0	.480	.864	.409
2001	ALDS	OAK	5	18	2	8	1	0	0	1	9	1	0	0	.476	.500	.444
2001	ALCS	SEA	5	17	0	2	0	0	0	2	2	2	2	0	.200	.118	.118
2001	WS	ARI	7	27	3	4	0	0	1	1	7	0	6	0	.179	.259	.148
2002	ALDS	ANA	4	16	6	8	0	0	2	3	14	2	3	0	.526	.875	.500
2003	ALDS	MIN	4	14	2	6	0	0	1	1	9	4	2	1	.556	.643	.429
2003	ALCS	BOS	7	30	3	7	2	0	1	2	12	2	4	1	.281	.400	.233
2003	WS	FLA	6	26	5	9	3	0	0	2	12	1	7	0	.393	.462	.346
2004	ALDS	MIN	4	19	3	6	1	0	1	4	10	1	4	1	.350	.526	.316
2004	ALCS	BOS	7	30	5	6	1	0	0	5	7	6	2	1	.333	.233	.200
2005	ALDS	LAA	5	21	4	7	0	0	2	5	13	1	5	1	.348	.619	.333
2006	ALDS	DET	4	16	4	8	4	0	1	1	15	1	2	0	.529	.938	.500
2007	ALDS	CLE	4	17	0	3	0	0	0	1	3	0	4	0	.176	.176	.176
2009	ALDS	MIN	3	10	4	4	2	0	1	2	9	3	0	0	.538	.900	.400
2009	ALCS	LAA	6	27	5	7	0	0	2	3	13	6	5	0	.394	.481	.259
2009	WS	PHI	6	27	5	11	3	0	0	1	14	1	6	0	.429	.519	.407
2010	ALDS	MIN	3	14	0	4	0	0	0	1	4	0	3	1	.286	.286	.286
2010	ALCS	TEX	6	26	2	6	3	1	0	1	11	2	7	0	.286	.423	.231
Career	14 ALDS		56	222	37	78	11	1	10	24	121	22	38	5	.410	.545	.351
Career	9 ALCS		53	221	32	57	10	2	7	24	92	28	40	8	.340	.416	.258
Career	7 WS		38	156	32	50	9	1	3	9	70	13	39	4	.384	.449	.321
Career	30 SERIES		147	599	101	185	30	4	20	57	283	63	117	17	.377	.472	.309

FIELDING, REGULAR SEASON (GAMES AS SHORTSTOP)

SEASON	G	TC	PO	A	E	DP	FPCT
1995	15	53	17	34	2	7	.962
1996	157	710	244	444	22	83	.969
1997	159	719	244	457	18	87	.975
1998	148	625	223	393	9	82	.986
1999	158	632	226	392	14	86	.978
2000	148	610	238	348	24	78	.961
2001	150	570	212	343	15	68	.974
2002	156	600	219	367	14	69	.977
2003	118	444	159	271	14	51	.968
2004	154	678	273	392	13	96	.981
2005	157	731	262	454	15	96	.979
2006	150	610	214	381	15	81	.975
2007	155	607	199	390	18	104	.970
2008	148	579	220	347	12	69	.979
2009	150	554	206	340	8	75	.986
2010	151	553	182	365	6	94	.989
Career	2274	9275	3338	5718	219	1226	.976

CAREER RANKINGS AS A YANKEE

1st: At-bats (9,322; 13th in A.L.), hits (2,926; 11th in A.L.); as shortstop: games (2,274), total chances (9,275), putouts (3,338), assists (5,718), double plays (1,226), fielding percentage (virtual tie with Bucky Dent at .976, 1st among Yankees with at least 50 games as shortstop)

2nd: Games (2,295; 1st, Mantle, 2,401), doubles (468; 1st, Gehrig, 534), stolen bases (323; 1st, Ricky Henderson, 326), strikeouts (1,572; 1st, Mantle, 1,710; 9th in A.L.)

3rd: Runs (1,685; 1st, Ruth, 1,959; 12th in A.L.)

4th: Total bases (4,218; 1st, Ruth, 5,131)

5th: Batting average (.314; 1st, Ruth, .349; 12th in A.L.)

6th: Bases on balls (948; 1st, Ruth, 1,852)

9th: Runs batted in (1,135; 1st, Gehrig, 1,995)

10th: Home runs (234; 1st, Ruth, 659)

13th: On-base percentage (.385; 1st, Ruth, .479)

AWARDS AND ACHIEVEMENTS

1994: Baseball America Minor League Player of the Year (Columbus)

1996: Rookie of the Year

1997: 1st in singles and assists as SS

1998: All-Star*, 1st in runs scored and singles, 3rd in M.V.P. vote

1999: All-Star*, 1st in hits, 2nd in batting average, runs scored, triples and singles

2000: World Series M.V.P., All-Star M.V.P., 2nd in singles

2001: All-Star*

2002: All-Star*, 2nd in singles

2004: Gold Glove, All-Star, 1st in putouts as SS

2005: Gold Glove, 2nd in runs scored, singles, assists and putouts as SS

2006: Gold Glove, Silver Slugger, All-Star, 2nd in M.V.P. vote, batting average, runs scored and singles, Hank Aaron award (best hitter)

2007: Silver Slugger, All-Star

2008: Silver Slugger, All-Star

2009: Gold Glove, Silver Slugger, All-Star, 1st in fielding percentage as SS, 2nd in hits and singles, 3rd in M.V.P. vote, Hank Aaron award (best hitter), M.L. Roberto Clemente award (community work), Sports Illustrated's Sportsman of the Year

2010: Gold Glove, All-Star, 1st in fielding percentage as SS, 2nd in runs scored

Note: All are American League honors except All-Star, M.V.P. award and votes, Clemente and Sports Illustrated; * = All-Star reserve player

ACKNOWLEDGMENTS

The New York Times sports pages have been a showcase for its talented writers and photographers, capturing Yankees action throughout every season and postseason.

Thanks to the following writers for their contributions: Jack Curry, Tyler Kepner, Buster Olney, Dave Anderson, George Vecsey, Harvey Araton, Claire Smith, Joe Lapointe, Ira Berkow, Ben Shpigel, Richard Sandomir, Murray Chass, Dave Caldwell, David Waldstein, Bruce Weber, Karen Crouse, Selena Roberts, Dan Barry, Pat Borzi, Michael S. Schmidt, Corey Kilgannon, Joe Brescia, Anna Kisselgoff, Alan Schwarz and Joshua Robinson.

Thanks to the following photographers for their contributions: Barton Silverman, Richard Perry, Chang W. Lee, Fred Conrad, Vincent Laforet, G. Paul Burnett, Ozier Muhammad, Marilynn K. Yee, Librado Romero, James Estrin, Larry Morris, Chip Litherland, Uli Seit, Tim Shaffer, Blake J. Discher, Carl Skalak, Keith Bedford and Robert Caplin.

We also wish to thank the following for their photographic contributions: Paul Aiken, Bobby Bank, Al Bello, Jemal Countess, Stephen Dunn, Dana Edelson, Frank Franklin II, Ron Frehm, Stan Honda, Harry How, Kevin Kane, Mark Lennihan, Saul Loeb, Jim McIsaac, Arnaldo Magnani, Al Messerschmidt, Ronald C. Modra, Steve Nesius, Chris O'Meara, Doug Pensinger, Gene J. Puskar, Robert Riger, Mark Rucker, Rick Stewart, Jason Szenes, Chris Trotman, Jeffrey Ufberg, Toru Yamanaka and Matt York.

Thanks to Richard Slovak, who read through thousands of articles about Derek Jeter that have run in The Times, from which he, Tyler Kepner and Alex Ward made the final selections. Vincent Alabiso selected the photographs, and Phyllis Collazo helped with the picture research. Thanks also to Eric Himmel, Steve Tager, Anet Sirner-Bruder, Michelle Ishay, Ankur Ghosh, Kara Strubel and Kathleen Go at Abrams and to Sam Eckersley, Stuart Rogers, Jane Huschka and Eliza Cerdeiros at RED Design.

Jeter poses with Brooke Goldfarb, 11, as she, her mother, Cori, and sisters Paige, 8, left, and Remi, 7, juggle their cell phone cameras in the Yankees dugout at Legends Field in Tampa, Fla., during the first day of full team workouts at spring training, *Feb. 20, 2007. Photo: Chip Litherland for The New York Times*

INDEX

Page numbers in italics refer to illustrations.

Editorial Direction: Alex Ward

Editor: Richard Slovak

Photo Editor: Vincent Alabiso

Photo Researcher: Phyllis Collazo

Designer: Rogers Eckersley Design (RED)

Production Manager: Anet Sirna-Bruder

Library of Congress Cataloging-in-Publication Data

Derek Jeter : from the pages of the New York Times /
introduction by Tyler Kepner.

p. cm.

Includes index.

ISBN 978-0-8109-9656-4 (alk. paper)

1. Jeter, Derek, 1974-   2. Baseball players--United States--Biography.

3. New York Yankees (Baseball team)   4. Baseball--New York (State)--New York.

I. New York times.

GV865.J48D45 2011

796.357092--dc22

[B]

2010045757

Printed and bound in U.S.A.

10 9 8 7 6 5 4 3 2 1

Abrams Books are available at special discounts when purchased in
quantity for premiums and promotions as well as fundraising or
educational use. Special editions can also be created to specification.
For details, contact specialmarkets@abramsbooks.com or the address below.

THE ART OF BOOKS SINCE 1949

115 West 18th Street
New York, NY 10011
www.abramsbooks.com

EDITOR'S NOTE:

Many of the selections in this book are
abridged. To read the complete articles,
visit http://www.nytimes.com and search
using the publication dates cited here.

Pages 2-3: Early arrivals in the stands watch
the Yankees hold their first workout at the new
Yankee Stadium, before beating the Chicago Cubs,
7-4, in an exhibition game, *April 2, 2009.*
Photo: Barton Silverman, The New York Times

Pages 4-5: Jeter warms up on deck at Yankee Stadium,
April 3, 2008.
Photo: Chris Trotman, Getty Images

Page 7: Jeter bats in the first inning of Game 6 of the
World Series at Yankee Stadium, *Nov. 4, 2009.*
Photo: Chang W. Lee, The New York Times